"The *Outside-the-Box Recovery Workbook* is amazing. Innovative, fresh, thorough, and thoughtful, it provides a solid action-plan for recovery that is not only extremely helpful but also extremely engaging. Dr. Kim Rosenthal knows her stuff. Whether you are a veteran substance abuse counselor or brand new to recovery, this workbook is a must-have tool for those who fight the disease of addiction." -Randy Withers, MA, LCMHC, LCAS

"Dr. Rosenthal combines her years of clinical expertise and wisdom with humor to create an invaluable *Outside-the-Box Recovery Workbook* edutainment for use by addiction recovery professionals and the general public alike. I highly recommend this manual, which gives practical, easy-to-follow teachings, exercises and musings for use in the recovery field." -Tracy Latz, MD, MS, MhD

"One of the topics I've been trying to encourage in my clients is staying motivated in treatment and recovery. I've been trying to find new ways to keep them going after they feel better, hoping they don't get complacent. This is why I'm so excited about this workbook. I have been looking for just this type of interaction for recovery to spice things up. Crossword puzzles and word finds that are FUN to do in master recovery, to help them stay connected? This is amazing. I would love to implement them into my curriculum. Bravo Bravo!!!!!" -Charlotte K Prather, SUDC

"The *Outside-the-Box Recovery Workbook* invokes cognitive activities and response in a unique format that my clients may not have experienced in previous treatment. Behavior change is not glossed over as an easy endeavor but a more realistic, difficult one – but I like the way Dr. Rosenthal utilizes humor to lighten the effects of self-reflection. I also love the section on dealing with relapse. No drama, no blaming, just a down to earth, matter-of-fact evaluation of what caused the lapse and how to move on with the business of recovery." -Lisa Appleby, BSW, QP, CADC-R

"Buy this book! For yourself, for a client, for a friend or anyone you know struggling with substance use disorder/addiction. This workbook allows a person to find help in working through their own journey in recovery. It can be used individually or as a homework tool for your client. Excellent resource!" -Carmen M. Givens, MSW, LCSW, LCAS

"Dr. Kim Rosenthal's book is an excellent tool for substance use disorder patients to utilize in recovery. Her use of satire throughout the workbook allows for patients to find humor in recovery while understanding the importance of basic recovery concepts. It is easy to follow, so patients have the option to work through it on their own, or it can be utilized in a therapeutic session with others." -Sherie Schaffer, ADC, LPC-S, NCC

"As a family physician, I've long searched for the perfect patient education resource, handouts or workbook to assist patients with addiction recovery and associated mental health issues. My prayers were answered when I found the unconventional, intriguing and useful *Outside-the-Box Recovery Workbook* by Kim Rosenthal MD. The author is highly qualified to write such a book since she is a psychiatrist and has worked with recovery and addiction in all capacities as part of her professional career. This workbook is well-written in an informal, friendly, laid back and at times, comic style, although the subject matter and information are serious and ask the reader to be introspective, to seriously review their behaviors and choices. I recommend this resource for any medical provider and anyone who is seeking help from addiction or knows a loved one who may benefit by having this book nearby." -Lisa M Lorelli, DO

"I'm a peer support specialist and have worked on my own recovery over the past ten years, which consists of over 20+ different detoxes, treatment facilities, and hospitals, everything from 12-step based, work-based, and spiritual-based to a combination of all three. From the jokes to the coloring material, the *Outside-the-Box Recovery Workbook* has the answers to questions that people needing recovery need to ask. This workbook has material I have never encountered in a workbook at the 20 plus places I've been. I believe this book can be very beneficial to those in long-term treatment." -Nathan Ray, Peer Support Specialist

"As I was going through the *Outside-the-Box Recovery Workbook*, I was thinking of different clients I see that could definitely benefit from using this manual. I am familiar with a lot of the content, which made it easy to read and understand. The progression of the workbook is nice. It starts off simple, for someone in early recovery and goes all the way to relapse prevention. I think the time frame (30 days) is just enough to help someone get stabilized in a treatment program. I often encounter clients who upon entering treatment don't want to attend group sessions but will ask if I have a workbook they can work on their own, and this book would be perfect for that. I would definitely use this workbook at my place of work. I can't wait until it is on the market and we have full access." -Josefina Pérez, LSAA

"I used some of the worksheets with inpatient clients at the hospital who are in pre-contemplation/contemplation towards addressing their substance use disorder. They have enjoyed the pages and I have found them useful for facilitating conversations to help increase their motivation. I like that the work engages the creative side of the brain and spans appropriate comprehension level of multiple groups...." -Julie Bowers-Pryor, MA, MSSW, LCADC, CSW

The Outside-the-Box Recovery Workbook

**ILLUSTRATED, FUN AND PROFESSIONAL HANDOUTS
FOR CLINICIANS AND
PEOPLE IN EARLY RECOVERY**

Motivational Interviewing
Relapse Prevention
Cognitive Behavioral Therapy
Dialectical Behavioral Therapy
Coping and Life Skill Training
Matrix Model
Narrative Therapy
Art Therapy
Expressive Therapy
Positive Psychology
12-Step Programming
And more!

**KIM ROSENTHAL, MD
KIMROSENTHALMD.COM**

The Outside-the-Box Recovery Workbook
*Illustrated, Fun, and Professional Handouts for Clinicians
and People in Early Recovery*

Copyright 2021 by Kim Rosenthal, MD
All rights reserved

Kim Rosenthal, MD
Rosenthal Publishing LLC
P.O Box 2783
Lenoir, NC 28645
kimrosenthalmd.com

The information in this publication is not intended to be a substitution for consultation with a health care professional. Individual health concerns should be assessed by a qualified clinician.

Care has been taken to confirm the accuracy of the information presented. However, the author is not responsible for errors or any consequences from application of this information, and she makes no warranty, expressed or implied, for the contents in this book.

All names and events described in this workbook are fictional. Any likeness to real people is coincidental.

Permission is granted for the purchaser to photocopy individual handouts in limited number for use with clients. Except as noted, no parts of this book may be reproduced, translated, stored in a retrieval system, or transmitted, in any form or by any means, electronic, mechanical, recording, or smoke signals, without written permission from the author.

Author, illustrator, and interior designer: Kim Rosenthal, MD
Cover artist: Kim Rosenthal, MD

First Edition printed August 2021.

Library of Congress Cataloging-in-Publication Data

Rosenthal, Kim (2021). *The Outside-the-Box Recovery Workbook: Illustrated, Fun, and Professional Handouts for Clinicians and People in Early Recovery*. Lenoir, NC: Rosenthal Publishing.

ISBN 978-1-7369741-0-0
LCCN 2021906925

Printed in the United States.

This workbook is dedicated to::

My husband, the center of my universe, who encourages me to keep going and keep writing no matter what.

Everyone in my support team -- family, friends, colleagues, subscribers, book-buyers, website visitors, Facebook companions, and the hundreds of substance use disorder counselors who helped sustain me throughout this project.

My patients, who shared their experiences, from tragedy to unbelievable triumph, and taught me more about life than books could ever teach.

"The creation of something new
is not accomplished by the
intellect but by the play instinct
acting from inner necessity."

-Carl Jung

I'm your official Welcome Wagon.

Hello there!

WELCOME

TO

RECOVERY

CONTENTS

WELCOME/INSTRUCTIONS	1
RELAPSE PREVENTION PLAN	3
Relapse Prevention Plan	5
(Ludicrous) Rescue Card	7
Choose Your Direction	8
DAYS 1-30	9
Day 1. Why Did You Quit? (Letter)	11
Day 2. Opinions and Trivia (Word Search)	14
Day 3. The YOU Before It All Happened (Scenario, Dialogue)	18
Day 4. The Effects of Substance Use Disorders (Pie Chart)	20
Day 5. Describing Addiction Through Art (Drawing)	23
Day 6. Relationship with Addiction I (Movie)	25
Day 7. Relationship with Addiction II (Movie)	27
Take a Break Please (Pick a Cartoon)	*29*
Day 8. What is Recovery? (Scenario)	30
Day 9. Identifying Triggers (Scenario/Word Search)	32
Day 10. Dealing with Unavoidable Triggers (Scenario)	34
Day 11. Getting Past Cravings I (A Joke Ha Ha)	37
Day 12. Getting Past Cravings II (Crossword Puzzle)	41
Take a Break Please (Recovery Maze)	*44*
Day 13. Grieving the Loss of Addiction (Letter)	45
Day 14. Grieving the Loss of Addiction (Ritual)	48
Day 15. Grieving the Loss of Addiction (Wish List)	50
Solve This Code Please (Cryptogram)	*51*
Day 16. Introducing Change (Lyrics)	53
Day 17. Change What You Do (Scenario)	56

Day 18. Change How You Talk (Follow the Arrows) 59
Day 19. Change and Alter Ego I (Creativity) 61
Day 20. Change and Alter Ego II (Scenarios) 64
Please Solve This Puzzle (Sober Word Search) 67
Day 21. Addiction's Effect on Others (Art) 68
Day 22. The Interview: Recognizing Mistakes (Scenario) 69
Day 23. After the Interview: Mistakes and Hope (Newspaper) 72
Take a Break Please (Tips for Recovery Word Search) 75
Day 24. Mistakes Without Forgiveness (Scenario) 76
Day 25. Self-forgiveness (Letter) 79
Day 26. People in Your Life (Diagram) 81
Day 27. Making Friends (Scenario & Word Search) 83
Day 28. The New YOU in Recovery (Follow the Arrows) 87
Day 29. The Bucket List (Comic) 89
Day 30. Your Future in Recovery (Art) 93
What to Do When You Finish This Book 97

RESOURCES FOR YOUR JOURNEY **99**

APPENDICES **101**

Appendix A. Dealing with Relapse 103
Coloring (Breathe Now) *104*
Appendix B. A Note to Professionals / Worksheet Recommendations 110
Appendix C. Answers 118

REFERENCES **125**

ABOUT THE AUTHOR **127**

FINAL WORDS **128**

ABOUT THE READER **129**

"Think Outside-the-Box" Coloring 131

WELCOME

You've reached *The Outside-the-Box Recovery Workbook*. We're going to take you on a 30-day journey into the world of sobriety, where hard work meets odd scenarios, alter egos, art therapy, movie-writing, cartoons, and the occasional joke. That includes:

- Relapse prevention
- Dealing with cravings and triggers
- Understanding change
- Processing mistakes
- Grieving the loss of addiction
- Making friends
- Creating a sober identity, and more!

Whether you're a seasoned provider sharing this book with clients or someone new to recovery, please join us for the trip of a lifetime!

INSTRUCTIONS

1. Buy yourself an *Outside-the-Box Recovery Workbook*. If you're reading this, it means you've probably already found a copy. We're pleased with your progress.

2. Approach the book with a pen. If the workbook runs off, chase it. These manuals are a lively bunch, but they do tame once they know who's boss. Be a gentle boss.

3. Use your pen to complete the exercises. Make sure to answer everything in *writing*. Nope, it doesn't count otherwise. There are questions to be considered, drawings to be drawn, and doodles to be doodled. Please ignore all mistakes and laugh at all jokes.

4. Make sure to complete the Relapse Prevention Plan first (pages 3-8) before moving onto Day 1 (page 11). Now turn the page and go go go!

EXTRA INFORMATION

→ *Just to confuse everyone, terms like substance abuse, addiction, "using," chemical dependency, and substance use disorder are used interchangeably throughout this book. In true life, they have different meanings. See Day 2 (page 14) for details.*

→ *See Appendix A (page 103) if you slip up or relapse.*

→ *See Appendix B (page 110) if you're a medical professional. Here you'll find background and recommendations.*

→ *See Appendix C (page 118) for answers to all brainteasers and puzzles.*

→ *Don't forget to complete the "About the Reader" card at the end of the book (page 129). Thanks!*

Relapse Prevention Plan

RELAPSE PREVENTION PLAN (P1)

1. WHAT ARE THE WARNING SIGNS THAT SUGGEST YOU'RE AT RISK FOR RELAPSE?

- ☐ Over-confidence, no need for treatment
- ☐ Start romanticizing past drug use
- ☐ Believe "I can drink/use a small amount"
- ☐ Isolating, irritability, cockiness
- ☐ Feeling unable to cope
- ☐ Other warning signs:
- ☐ Feeling stressed and overwhelmed
- ☐ Starting to lie to people I care about
- ☐ Becoming defensive around drug use
- ☐ Loss of interest in hobbies/activities
- ☐ Obsessing with pills and medications

If any of these warning signs are present, reach out for help now.

2. WHAT ARE YOUR TRIGGERS? WHAT CAUSES YOU TO HAVE CRAVINGS TO USE?

- ☐ Loneliness, frustration, exhaustion
- ☐ Depression, anxiety, or mania
- ☐ Situations where drugs are available
- ☐ Social isolation
- ☐ Other triggers:
- ☐ Relationship problems
- ☐ Things going too well
- ☐ Situations where I used to use/drink
- ☐ Hunger and boredom

If you feel yourself responding to a trigger, reach out for help now.

3. WHAT ARE YOUR REASONS FOR STAYING IN RECOVERY?

What bad things could happen if you relapse?

- ☐ Hurt family and friends
- ☐ Relapse after long period in recovery
- ☐ Hate myself afterwards
- ☐ Health problems
- ☐ Experience bad effects of drug
- ☐ Other problems with using:
- ☐ Become homeless
- ☐ Lose custody of my kid(s)
- ☐ Legal problems/jail or prison
- ☐ Potentially die
- ☐ Potentially hurt or kill somebody

What are the benefits of staying clean and sober?

- ☐ Make others proud
- ☐ Recognize I've overcome so much
- ☐ Get my self-esteem back
- ☐ Be a good parent
- ☐ Go back to school/do well in school
- ☐ Travel, grow, learn, thrive
- ☐ Other dreams I can achieve if clean/sober:
- ☐ Get clean time under my belt
- ☐ Be healthy and clear-minded
- ☐ Stay out of jail/avoid probation
- ☐ Find a job/do well at work
- ☐ Find my own place
- ☐ In time have people trust me again

(Turn to page 6)

RELAPSE PREVENTION PLAN (P2)

4. PROTECT YOURSELF AGAINST CRAVINGS. MAKE THINGS SAFER:

- ☐ Tell others I have quit
- ☐ Avoid/deal with trigger
- ☐ Avoid access to drugs/alcohol
- ☐ Limit access to money
- ☐ Other ideas:
- ☐ Decide not to use today
- ☐ Avoid former hangouts/using friends
- ☐ Talk regularly to therapist or doctor
- ☐ Go to 12-step meetings

5. USE SURVIVAL STRATEGIES TO FORTIFY YOURSELF:

- ☐ ***Review page 1 of this plan***
- ☐ Keep a gratitude list
- ☐ Journal or write a meaningful letter
- ☐ Pray or go to church
- ☐ Problem-solve/approach differently
- ☐ Eat healthy and exercise
- ☐ Other ideas:
- ☐ Call someone I trust
- ☐ Meditate/do mindfulness exercises
- ☐ Change behavior/act differently
- ☐ Make a list of my strengths
- ☐ Adapt to situations I can't change
- ☐ Relax muscles/get a massage

6. FOCUS ON HEALTHY BEHAVIORS/DISTRACTION/FUN:

- ☐ Google *Google Pacman*→"I'm feeling lucky"
- ☐ Google *do a barrel roll*
- ☐ Go hiking
- ☐ Watch a TV show or good movie
- ☐ Play with a pet
- ☐ Explore *https://elgoog.im/*
- ☐ Write a letter of forgiveness
- ☐ Read a comedy or comic book
- ☐ Do a puzzle or brainteaser
- ☐ Visit *Google Sky* to explore universe
- ☐ Google *Google Sphere*→"I'm feeling lucky"
- ☐ Other ideas:
- ☐ Play *https://elgoog.im/breakout*
- ☐ Volunteer to help somebody
- ☐ Google *askew*
- ☐ Visit a bookstore
- ☐ Go to a theater/movie
- ☐ Google *Zergrush* → "I'm feeling lucky"
- ☐ Draw or color in a coloring book
- ☐ Listen to music
- ☐ Google *Google gravity*→"I'm feeling lucky"
- ☐ Search online, "fun things to do"
- ☐ Visit kimrosenthalmd.com

7. CRAVINGS WON'T GO AWAY?
Repeat above process. But if you're losing the battle, call SAMHSA's national crisis/relapse prevention hotline at 1.800.662.4357.

RELAPSE PREVENTION PLAN (P3)
THE (LUDICROUS) RESCUE CARD

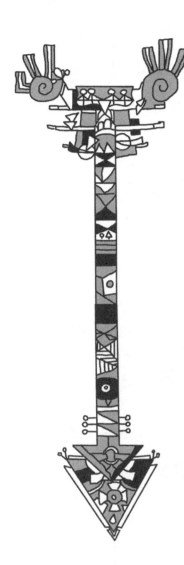

Below you'll find the (*Ludicrous*) *Rescue Card*. We're not sure who wrote it, but they were in a really bad mood when they did.

INSTRUCTIONS:
(1) Read card. See below.
(2) Shake head and throw card away.
(3) Walk away.
(4) Come back and fish card out of garbage.
(5) Make 10 copies and put them in your wallet.
(6) Offer a card to any person who tempts or triggers you.
(7) Don't say anything. Just point to card.
(8) Nod knowingly.
(9) Observe as other person runs away.

Never mind.
Maybe it's best to just leave the card in the trash.

← cut here →

The Ludicrous Rescue Card:
WARNING: I JUST QUIT USING DRUGS AND ALCOHOL.

1. Please don't talk to me. Everything you say will frustrate me.
2. Please keep your distance. Step too close and I just might clout you.*
3. Thanks. Have a super day!

---

*__Small print:__ We do not condone violence in any form. The person who wrote the Ludicrous Rescue Card should be ashamed of themselves. There is never a good reason to clout others, no matter how many cards you have to give them.

RELAPSE PREVENTION (P4)

CHOOSE YOUR DIRECTION

Not sure where to go next? Start with Day 1 or choose from the following:

Days 1-30

DAY 1. WHY DID YOU QUIT?

PURPOSE OF THIS WORKSHEET:

- To remember why you quit
- Really, to remember why you quit!

WHY'D YOU STOP USING?

Or, rather, why did you choose recovery? You've been asked this before, but for recovery to work, you have to revisit this question frequently. No worries! To make things easier, here's a list of common reasons. Check all that apply.

REASONS TO GIVE UP DRUGS/ALCOHOL	
Check the options that play/played a role in your decision to quit.	
Family/friends	
☐ To start a new relationship	☐ To care for my loved one(s)
☐ To be a better partner	☐ To be a better parent
☐ To be a good example for others	☐ To keep custody of my kids
☐ To be a good friend	☐ To have a healthy pregnancy
Lifestyle	
☐ To stay in school/improve my grades	☐ To keep/do well at my job
☐ To start at a new school/college	☐ To start a new career

☐ To pass drug tests	☐ To advance in the world
☐ To avoid homelessness	☐ To maintain housing
☐ To be financially independent	☐ To save money
☐ To take care of my family financially	☐ To avoid (more) debt

Health

☐ To get into better shape	☐ To avoid getting sick
☐ To avoid mixing drugs with medications	☐ To avoid bad highs
☐ To avoid withdrawal or detox	☐ To prevent overdoses and ER visits

Legal Issues

☐ To fulfill the terms of my probation/parole	☐ To avoid jail/prison
☐ To avoid problems with the law	☐ To avoid DUIs

Psychological Issues

☐ To improve my self-confidence	☐ To reach for my dreams and goals
☐ To remember who I am	☐ To live a fulfilling, worthwhile life

Drug behaviors

☐ To avoid more consequences	☐ To let my brain heal
☐ To not get hurt	☐ To have free time to do other stuff
☐ To stop hurting others	☐ To not let drugs control me

Add your reasons.

IMAGINE YOU'VE BEEN CLEAN FOR A MONTH.

It's been a *horrible* month. Your parents aren't talking to you. Your boss gave you the cold shoulder. Your dog passed away. You just learned you're being evicted. The cravings are overwhelming. You haven't relapsed, but your brain is circling in a bad place.

Write a letter to yourself offering advice, hope, a pep-talk. Focus on why you chose recovery. Use the space below (or a separate sheet of paper) and be specific.

REFLECTION

Reread your letter. How does it make you feel? If your response is "I'd still want to use," what can you add to remind yourself why you chose recovery? "Before" and "After" pictures? Photos of your kids? A description of who you want to be? Really, what gives you strength and direction during those vulnerable moments? Add this to your letter. Use an additional piece of paper if you need it.

When finished, go over this worksheet again. There are a number of therapy dogs in the pictures. How many can you find? See Appendix C for the answer.

DAY 2. OPINIONS AND TRIVIA

PURPOSE OF THIS WORKSHEET:

- To explore the complexities of substance use disorders
- To test what you know about random trivia

OPINION. Read the following questions and tell us what you think. Write your answers.

1. Are substance abuse, substance dependence, substance use, addiction, chemical dependency, drug use, drug abuse, and substance use disorders the same thing? (Hint: *The answer is NO, but these terms are used interchangeably in this book*).

2. Do addicts need to "hit bottom" to accept treatment?

3. Is forcing somebody into treatment effective?

4. Is addiction a disease or a choice?

5. Does chemical dependency hurt the brain permanently?

See the answers at the end of this worksheet.

TRUE / FALSE

TRUE OR FALSE. Decide whether the following are true or false.

1. _____ Some cigarettes made in China contain insect eggs and human feces.

2. _____ Globally alcohol causes one death per minute.

3. _____ In California, it's illegal to give wine to cows.

4. _____ Overdose on cocaine can cause stroke or brain damage, potentially leaving you dependent on others to feed and toilet you for the rest of your life. You could also have a heart attack, seizure, kidney failure, problems breathing, or death. (Please don't use cocaine.)

5. _____ Alcohol withdrawal can kill you.

6. _____ Using methamphetamine on a long-term basis can fry your brain permanently.

7. _____ Carfentanyl, similar to the opioid Fentanyl, is so toxic that Narcan (a medication used to reverse opioid overdose) often doesn't work.

8. _____ Bath salts can turn you into a cannibal.

9. _____ Spiders exposed to weed build artistic and beautiful webs.

10. _____ Long-term alcohol use can cause vitamin deficiencies, anemia, pink elephants, problems finding the ground, pancreatitis, liver disease, cancer, and excessive hair growth.

ANSWERS TO QUESTIONS

1. These terms aren't the same. Addiction is a word that describes any problematic, compulsive behavior, like heroin use disorder or gambling. Substance use disorder occurs when a person is addicted to drugs or alcohol. The rest are informal words for different severities and

flavors of "substance use disorder." *For the purposes of this book, we use all terms interchangeably.* Just to upset people.
2. Opinions will vary. According to the psychiatric Bible (DSM V), substance use disorder can be mild, moderate, or severe. Persons from all stages are known to pursue treatment. However, Step One in the 12-Step Program describes loss of control over addiction as the major motivating factor; life is unmanageable. Does that mean hitting bottom? You decide.
3. Opinions will vary. Most people will say that "forcing" someone into treatment is useless. However, there are suggestions that "getting" someone away from drugs for an extended period of time can be helpful.
4. These days it's generally accepted that addiction is a disease. Most people don't wake up one day and think, "Yeah, I'm going to become an addict!" The inability to quit is actually a symptom of the disease. But people with chemical dependency can *choose* to get help. Confusing.
5. Drugs and alcohol injure the brain. With long-term use, the effects can be permanent. Some chemicals are more toxic than others.

ANSWERS TO TRUE AND FALSE
1. True.
2. False. Alcohol causes *six* deaths every minute.
3. Who knows? We couldn't find any evidence that it's illegal, but you shouldn't give wine to cows. Don't do it.
4. True.
5. True.
6. True. Methamphetamine is known to cause insanity/thinking problems.
7. True. Fentanyl and its derivatives are extremely dangerous. Carfentanyl is so potent and quick-acting that the person often dies even after Narcan is administered.
8. True. That's bath salts, the drug – not bath salts for the tub.
9. False. Spiders exposed to drugs, including marijuana, build twisted, incompetent webs.
10. False. Okay, most of this is true… except for the pink elephants and back hair. Problems finding the ground is indeed a symptom of alcohol use disorder related to vitamin deficiency.

REFLECTION

Drugs and alcohol cause problems, but people can overcome them. How? Identify 4 motivators or methods to get past addiction. Write them below before going onto the page.

Method/motivator #1	Method/motivator #2
Method/motivator #3	Method/motivator #4

word search

OVERCOMING DRUGS. There are hundreds of ways to quit using. Apart from rehab, twenty-six methods and motivators are listed below. Locate each in the word search puzzle.

D	D	C	A	M	P	R	A	L	S	N	O	I	T	A	C	U	D	E	S
G	T	H	T	F	Y	D	A	Y	P	R	O	G	R	A	M	D	R	H	N
S	E	D	E	C	I	D	E	T	R	S	H	I	N	T	O	F	Y	U	O
I	N	T	E	N	S	I	V	E	O	U	T	P	A	T	I	E	N	T	S
N	Y	O	H	D	G	Y	U	H	B	B	H	D	R	Y	J	N	N	F	I
T	T	D	A	E	E	T	H	Q	A	O	E	D	H	V	Y	R	O	E	R
E	E	D	G	C	L	C	G	H	T	X	E	E	E	E	T	S	C	D	P
R	I	F	S	N	C	P	U	H	I	O	N	T	T	H	E	R	A	P	Y
V	R	R	R	R	O	E	U	H	O	N	R	O	S	E	F	E	S	L	M
E	B	O	E	S	P	S	S	E	N	E	N	X	R	N	A	H	H	O	E
N	O	T	H	E	I	R	E	S	S	F	R	Q	E	R	S	T	O	S	T
T	S	C	E	P	N	E	N	N	T	U	S	I	H	T	G	O	N	R	H
I	E	O	N	L	G	H	R	R	E	O	T	U	H	H	N	P	E	T	A
O	S	D	R	E	S	L	S	S	U	H	D	N	U	H	I	L	S	L	D
N	O	E	E	E	K	U	H	O	N	L	S	R	O	G	K	E	T	N	O
P	O	E	G	N	I	F	R	U	S	E	G	R	U	D	E	H	Y	R	N
L	H	S	L	S	L	O	N	E	E	Y	R	L	S	G	E	O	N	S	E
E	C	Y	R	E	L	D	E	E	T	W	E	L	V	E	S	T	E	P	S
O	N	A	D	D	S	U	H	L	S	E	S	U	B	A	T	N	A	U	H
A	H	I	T	B	O	T	T	O	M	O	N	E	E	Y	R	O	N	L	S

Antabuse
Campral
Choose sobriety
Coping skills
Day program
Decide
Detox
Don't use
Education

Get help
Help others
Hit bottom
Honesty
Intensive Outpatient
Intervention
Methadone
No access to drugs
No cash

Probation
Prison
See doctor
Seeking Safety
Suboxone
Twelve Steps
Therapy
Urge surfing

(See Appendix C for answers)

DAY 3. THE YOU BEFORE IT ALL HAPPENED

PURPOSE OF THIS WORKSHEET:

- To examine who you were before you started using
- To see which parts of this younger version of you are worth carrying into the future

WHEN THE "PAST YOU" MEETS THE "PRESENT YOU"

1. You're walking down the street and bump into a former version of yourself, the "Past You" before you started using. Choose your reaction.

   a. You stop, hide, and observe from a distance.
   b. You avoid them at all costs.
   c. You walk up and introduce yourself but maintain strict boundaries.
   d. You walk by without acknowledging them.
   e. You rush at them with a warm embrace and shower them with kisses.
   f. You shoot them on sight.

2. Before you're able to react, the Past You waves and steps up beside you. What are they like?

   a. The Past You is naïve, innocent, vulnerable, and happy. They know nothing.
   b. The Past You is a jerk. Bad attitude, bad news, bad everything; they're the last person you want to talk to.
   c. This person is pained. Their life is horrible. They're desperate for escape.
   d. The Past You has incredible potential. They have dreams and goals and can succeed at anything they want.
   e. None of the above. Or all of the above. You're not sure.

3. The conversation begins:

   Past You: "Do I know you?"
   Present You: "No."
   Past You: "You look familiar."
   Present You: "No, I don't."
   Past You: "Wait..."
   Present You: "Okay, okay. If you must know, I'm the future version of you."
   Past You: "Oh!" They study you closely, an insightful look on their face.

   And that's how you come face-to-face with your past. Please move onto the next page.

4. What does the Past You think about the Present You? Are they disappointed, proud, confused? Why? Sorry, no multiple choice this time. Please answer below.

5. What are the Past You's dreams? Make a list and label each as abandoned, fulfilled, or still ongoing.

6. Meeting this younger version of yourself triggers the parent inside you, the part of you that's brimming over with advice. If you could give one piece of advice, what would it be?

REFLECTION

That's history shared, friendship formed, dreams remembered, and advice given. By now your past and present have talked for hours, sharing everything they need to share. They separate with a handshake, each returning to their own life.

What was the Past You like?

Chances are you've made enormous mistakes, but you've done amazing things too. You've experienced life. You've grown. You've changed, and now you're in recovery. What's improved over the years? What hasn't?

What parts of the past are worth carrying into the future? Are there any abandoned goals you'd like to pick up again?

DAY 4. THE EFFECTS OF USING

PURPOSE OF THIS WORKSHEET:

- To learn more about the effect chemical dependency had/has on your life
- To use this information to make things better

HOW HAS ADDICTION AFFECTED YOU?

Below you'll find a circle that's been cut up like a pie, each piece labeled with a separate part of your life. In each section, write a phrase about how things were before you quit.

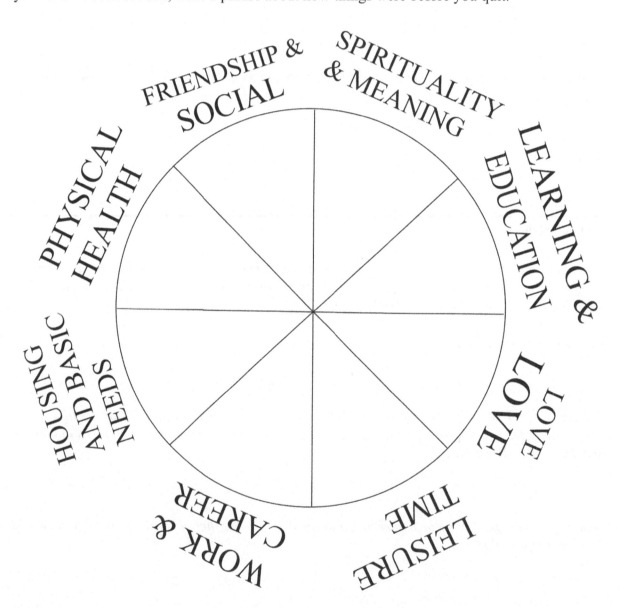

WHAT'S GOING WELL?

You're in recovery now, and things have changed. How happy are you with your life? Look at each category below and label between 1 and 10, 1 being most unhappy and 10 being happiest.

Argh, life is awful. ← → Yay, life is awesome!
1 2 3 4 5 6 7 8 9 10

_____Friendship and social life   _____Leisure time (creativity and fun)

_____Spirituality and meaning   _____Work and career

_____Learning and education   _____Housing and basic needs

_____Love love (yes, love!)   _____Physical health

REALLY, WHAT'S GOING WELL?

Here's another pie chart. Using the information above, draw a line across each section matching the number you chose. The lower the number, the closer to the center. Next, shade in the section under your line. Confused? See the next page for an example.

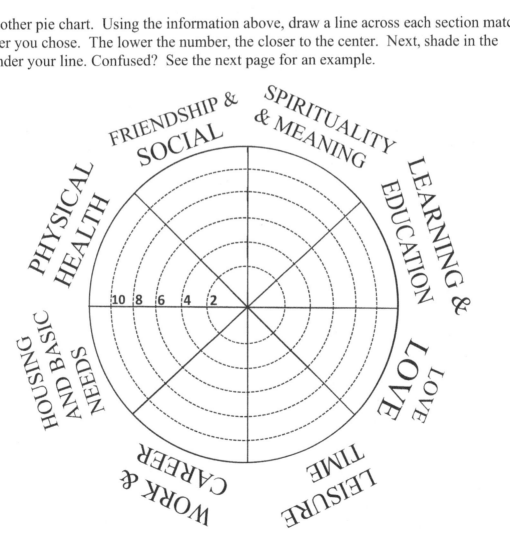

Here's an example. This is called a Wheel of Life, and it helps you see what's going right as well as places where there's room for improvement.

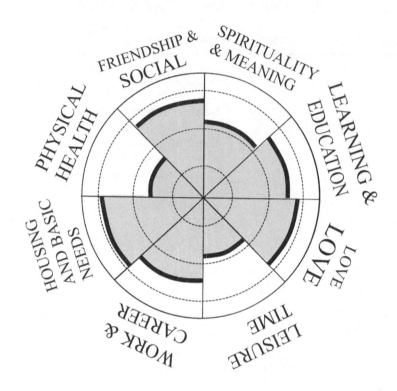

REFLECTION

Which two areas in your life were most affected when you were using? How?

Look at your Wheel of Life. How have things improved since you quit?

Which areas in your life still need work?

DAY 5. DESCRIBING ADDICTION THROUGH ART

PURPOSE OF THIS WORKSHEET:

- To explore chemical dependency in an intuitive, nonverbal way
- To draw something cool

WHAT DOES YOUR ADDICTION LOOK LIKE?

We've talked about addiction and how it has affected your life, but we still haven't answered the question, "What does chemical dependency look like?" Close your eyes and imagine addiction standing in front of you. How does it look? What is it doing? After a few minutes, draw what you see in the box below.

When finished, study the picture closely. Where is addiction? Is it beautiful or ugly? What is happening? Are you in the picture? Use the space surrounding the box to make notes and label what is what. Provide enough detail so that a stranger would understand what they see.

REFLECTION

How difficult was it to get into this project? (Most people find it very difficult!) How did it make you feel?

Using artwork to describe challenges can help make sense out of problems in new, nonverbal ways. What did you notice about addiction that you hadn't noticed before?

DAY 6. RELATIONSHIP WITH ADDICTION I

PURPOSE OF THIS WORKSHEET:

- To explore your relationship with substance use disorder
- To consider a positive outcome

Sometimes addiction is part of your identity, as if there's no line between where it ends and you begin. This worksheet helps you take a step back to see the relationship more clearly. You're about to create a movie. This involves choosing two actors (one for you, one for addiction), putting them in a room together, and watching what happens. We'll talk you through it.

THE "CHARACTER GENERATOR"

First, decide who represents you and who represents addiction.

Who plays **you**?	
Who plays **addiction**?	

Can't come up with ideas? No problem. The table below can help you create both characters. Read each question, then circle one of the answers.

THE CHARACTER GENERATOR	
Who/what plays **you** *in your movie?*	
Superman	A powerful angel
You, in recovery	Arnold Schwarzenegger (good guy)
The droid(s) from Star Wars	Angelina Jolie
Who/what plays **addiction**?	
Freddy Krueger	The Devil
You, using	The Terminator
The Borg from Star Trek	Hannibal Lecter

The Movies

Let's try again. Feel free to come up with your own ideas.

Who plays **you**?	
Who plays **addiction**?	

DEVELOP YOUR CHARACTER

You meet individually with both characters – YOU and ADDICTION – and ask each one to describe, in their own words, their take on the relationship between them. Fill in each box.

That's it! When ready, move onto the next worksheet for Part II.

DAY 7. RELATIONSHIP WITH ADDICTION II

PURPOSE OF THIS WORKSHEET:

- To better understand your relationship with chemical dependency
- To consider a positive outcome

Welcome back! It's time to bring your movie to life. Make sure to write your answers. Use additional paper if needed.

CHOOSE ONE OF THE FOLLOWING SCENES

  a. 12-step meeting
  b. Divorce court
  c. Outer space
  d. Empty room with a table, two chairs, and a gun
  e. Auditorium with an audience watching

NEXT, USE THE FOLLOWING QUESTIONS TO WRITE YOUR MOVIE.

a. The character that plays YOU is sitting alone in the scene you chose. Addiction makes an entrance. What's the first thing addiction does?

b. What happens next? Record the characters' first five minutes together.

c. A battle emerges. It might be an unfriendly chat, a punch or two, or a vicious sprawling fight. Describe the interaction in the space below.

d. The character who plays YOU wins. How do they do it? Write a few sentences bringing your film to an end.

Bravo, you've got your movie on paper! (Or you did what you could and now you're damned tired of trying). Either way, congratulations. Smile and pat yourself on the back.

Use your smartphone to make a movie. Shoot the scene from different angles. Have fun with lights and props. Include opening and closing music. Enjoy.

REFLECTION

Which title and actor name would you choose for your movie?

   a. *100 Meters to Rehab, starring Willy Go*
   b. *All You Need to Know About Quitting, starring Donna Trastim*
   c. *The Difficult Dilemma, starring Hugh Setback*
   d. *You have your own title and choice of actors and are offended at our recommendations*

What did you learn about addiction from this exercise?

What did you learn about yourself?

The 100,000-dollar question: How did it feel to win?

TAKE A BREAK
PLEASE

Relax your shoulders and take a break. Can you find (1) the one unique cartoon? (2) The cartoon that appears three times? See Appendix C for answers.

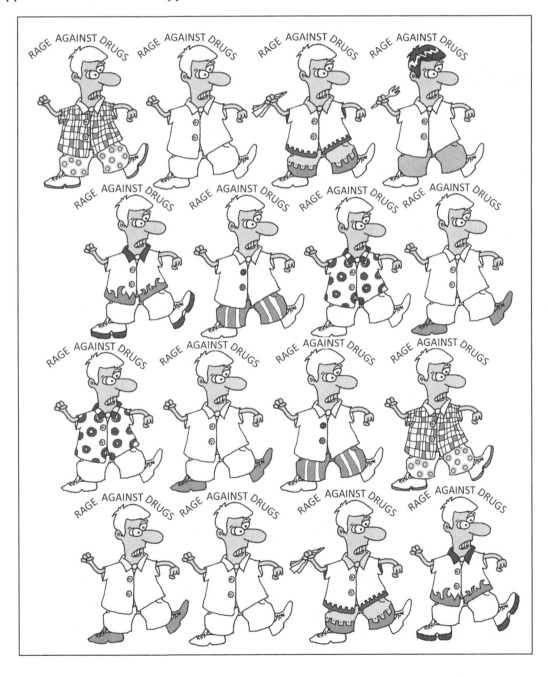

DAY 8. WHAT IS RECOVERY?

PURPOSE OF THIS WORKSHEET:

- To explore the meaning of recovery
- To understand the difference between abstinence and recovery

IMAGINE YOU WORK AT A COFFEE SHOP.

You're making a double shot vanilla mocha latte when a customer suddenly jumps up on a chair. He's a little fellow, but his voice thunders over the crowd. "I just quit using," he yells, "but I'm not in recovery, ha ha ha!"

You're about to grab the broom and shoo your visitor out the door when a second customer jumps up on a chair. It's an old lady. "I quit drinking 70 years ago," she yells, "but I'm not in recovery, ha ha ha!"

That's it, you think. You grab your phone and search the definition of *recovery*.

1. Out of the following definitions of RECOVERY, which ones are *false*?

    a. Recovery means a return to health after sickness. "The thief fell sick after he swallowed the stolen diamond, and *recovery* seemed far off."
    b. It's a place where people go after surgery. "The diamond was surgically removed. Now the thief is in the *recovery* room."
    c. It describes the regaining of something lost or taken away. "The police *recovered* the diamond from the hospital and returned it to me."
    d. In Italian, *recovere* translates to, "Now the diamond store refuses to take the smelly diamond back."
    e. Recovery is the act of covering something a second time. "Eventually I hid the diamond in the couch and *re-covered* the couch with a beautiful blue fabric."
    f. Recovery is when you quit drugs but don't pursue a new sober identity.
    g. Recovery is when you quit drugs and pursue a new sober identity.

2. What's going on with your customers? Which of the following is true?

a. The first customer is recovering from something other than addiction, like depression or herpes or leprosy.
b. The old lady is probably a dry drunk.
c. They're both confused.
d. Neither has looked up the definition of recovery lately.

3. Should you throw the two customers out of the café? What do you think?

a. Only if they don't order coffee.
b. Absolutely, but first search them for the stolen diamond.
c. Only if they can't pronounce "R-E-V-O-C-E-R-E" correctly.
d. Only if they recently re-covered their sofas.

ANSWERS

1. D and F are false. F is the definition of a "dry drunk," not recovery. E is unusual. The "right" definition of recovery, if there is one right answer, is G: for many, recovery is when you quit using and choose to be a cool sober person instead.
2. B. The answer isn't A because the first customer said he'd quit drugs – and said he's not in recovery. C and D are possibilities but not certain.
3. Opinions will vary. Frankly, all options are ridiculous.

REFLECTION

What does recovery mean to you? Write your definition below. Hint: It has something to do with G from Question #1.

How is quitting drugs/alcohol different to recovery? Hint: Look up "dry drunk" on Wikipedia.

How does a person know they've reached recovery? Hint: See Days 28 (page 87) and 30 (page 93) for ideas.

DAY 9. IDENTIFYING TRIGGERS

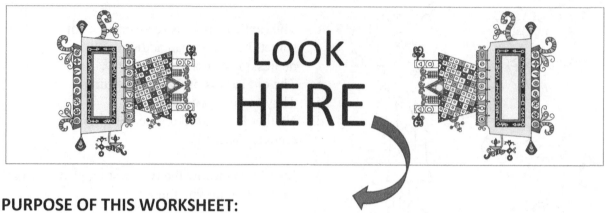

PURPOSE OF THIS WORKSHEET:

- To identify possible triggers
- To emphasize the importance of avoiding triggers

IDENTIFYING TRIGGERS

A trigger is anything that makes you want to use. Noisy neighbors and old using hangouts can be triggers. Thoughts, feelings, actions, sounds, and scents can also be triggers. If you really want to stay sober, it's important to identify your triggers and establish a game plan ahead of time to deal with them.

What are your main triggers?

Not sure? We have a list! Check the triggers that apply to you personally.

COMMON TRIGGERS THAT CAUSE RELAPSE	
Check all that sound familiar.	
☐ Relationship problems	☐ Social isolation
☐ Conflict with family	☐ Parties, clubs, and/or bars
☐ Seeing people use/drink	☐ Certain objects
☐ Certain people or places	☐ Certain thoughts or sensations
☐ Certain scents or sounds	☐ Certain memories or dreams
☐ Boredom	☐ Hunger or meals

☐ Coffee, tea, or other beverages	☐ Usually three months after I quit
☐ Access to money	☐ Break-up or divorce
☐ When lying seems okay	☐ Sex/intimacy
☐ Over-confidence / when doing well	☐ Trauma
☐ Thinking I can "use in moderation"	☐ When I can't cope
☐ Loneliness	☐ Being criticized or disrespected
☐ Depression or anxiety	☐ Rage/irritability
☐ Any old excuse	☐ I don't need a trigger

DEALING WITH TRIGGERS

Got a trigger in your life? We've got the perfect weapon. It's a simple 3-step process.

1) Avoid trigger.
2) Avoid trigger again!
3) If you can't avoid a trigger, take a deep breath and deal with it. We take on dealing with unavoidable triggers in the next handout.

REFLECTION

How many times can you find the words AVOID TRIGGER in the word search puzzle below?

"Avoid trigger"

A	A	R	E	G	G	I	R	T	D	I	O	V	A	A
A	V	O	R	A	V	O	I	D	T	R	I	V	V	R
R	O	O	A	E	T	D	I	O	V	A	O	A	E	E
E	I	A	I	T	G	N	O	P	E	I	E	G	S	G
G	D	V	U	D	O	G	O	N	D	A	G	T	T	G
G	T	O	M	B	T	S	I	T	R	I	G	R	A	I
I	R	I	T	R	I	R	R	R	R	T	R	I	Y	R
R	I	D	X	E	R	I	I	T	T	R	I	G	A	T
T	G	T	E	A	G	I	D	G	A	D	O	G	W	D
D	G	R	G	G	O	I	V	A	G	A	I	E	A	I
I	E	I	E	V	O	I	D	T	R	E	Y	O	Y	O
O	R	R	O	V	A	R	E	G	G	I	R	T	V	V
V	E	R	A	V	O	I	D	T	R	I	C	K	S	A
A	R	E	G	G	I	R	T	D	I	O	V	A	S	E

(See Appendix C for answers.)

DAY 10. DEALING WITH UNAVOIDABLE TRIGGERS

PURPOSE OF THIS WORKSHEET

- To find ways to deal with common triggers
- To recognize that addiction can touch anyone

WHAT ARE YOUR TRIGGERS?

A trigger is anything that makes you want to use. Jealous partners and dreams of using can be triggers. Thoughts, feelings, actions, sounds, and scents can also be triggers. If you really want to stay sober, it's important to identify your triggers and establish a game plan ahead of time to deal with them.

What are *your* triggers? List one trigger in each box below. If needed, refer to the list on Day 9 (page 28), "Common Triggers That Cause Relapse."

YOUR TRIGGERS
List one trigger in each box

1.

2.

3.

4.

→ For many people, hunger is a trigger

DEALING WITH TRIGGERS

Imagine you get a call. "They say you're the trigger expert," whispers a voice. You recognize her immediately. It's the mayor, the lovely Ms. Francisca De La Locura, and she sounds like she needs a friend.

"Mayor De La Locura, is that you?"

She laughs a friendly laugh and asks for the impossible. She's got these unavoidable triggers, and she needs help coming up with a plan to stay away from drugs and alcohol.

Wow, what a ridiculous introduction to trigger management, you think. "Okay, tell me the trigger, and I'll tell you how to handle it."

"No problem, sweetheart. I'll email you the list."

INSTRUCTIONS

Mayor De La Locura emails you the list. Go over her triggers and describe how you'd deal with each one. We completed the first one for you.

LIST OF UNAVOIDABLE TRIGGERS	
Describe how you'd handle each trigger.	
Trigger	*Ways to handle the trigger*
1. I bump into an old "using colleague" who invites me to a drug party.	Don't think. Just say NO! You've practiced saying NO hundreds of times, so many times it's become automatic. Keep doing it! (If you haven't practiced, start practicing now.)
2. I'm lonely and bored on a Friday night. Drugs will cheer me up.	
3. I'm thinking about the good old days. I miss the excitement of using.	
4. My cat died, and the grief is killing me. Drugs would ease the pain.	

5. They think I'm still using. What's the point of staying clean when everyone thinks I've relapsed?	

The mayor is satisfied with your answers. She asks you to vote for her in the upcoming election and hangs up the phone.

ANSWERS

Answers will vary, but here are some ideas.

1. Practice saying NO. You'll be saying it a lot in the future. *Recovery is precious and vulnerable. If you really want to stick with the plan, you must protect your recovery at all costs, and this means saying NO to triggers like drug parties.*
2. Call a sober friend! Go to a movie, meeting, mall, museum… there are a thousand healthy things you can do instead of sitting at home bored and lonely.
3. Don't forget how using messed you up. Don't glorify drugs. For more info, see Day 18 (page 59).
4. Learn ways to deal with painful emotion that don't involve using. Remind yourself grief takes time. Distract yourself. Reach out for help.
5. Maintain integrity. Don't relapse over someone else's stupidity!

REFLECTION

Imagine Ms. Locura had to deal with your triggers. For each of the four triggers you described earlier in this worksheet, what advice would you give her?

DAY 11. GETTING PAST CRAVINGS I

PURPOSE OF THIS WORKSHEET:

- To identify ways to get past cravings
- Repeat: To identify ways to get past cravings!

DEALING WITH CRAVINGS QUIZ

Choose the correct answer. There might be more than one.

1. How do you handle cravings?

    a. Just put up with them until they go away.
    b. Give in and relapse every time.
    c. I have superb coping skills which I activate every time cravings crop up.
    d. I've got a system. Yep. It's a secret.

2. Which of the following is false?

    a. Men are more likely to have an addiction than women.
    b. More than 65% of people in prison or jail meet the criteria for substance use disorder.
    c. Less than 20% of addicts and alcoholics get treatment.
    d. DUI lawyers never have any drug or alcohol problems. Ever. Never.

3. What are the best ways to handle something that makes you want to use?

    a. Combine it with an urge.
    b. Avoid it.
    c. Expose yourself to it over and over until it doesn't bother you.
    d. If it's bad, call a safe person.

ANSWERS

1. Answers will vary. Hopefully you chose C. A is acceptable, and D too, assuming your secret is a good one.
2. D. All the others are true.
3. B and D are best. Avoid A. C typically doesn't work, not in the beginning.

Please move onto the next page.

A CRAVING IS A STRONG DESIRE TO DO DRUGS OR ALCOHOL.
To help you deal with cravings, we've prepared the following flow chart. Please enjoy.

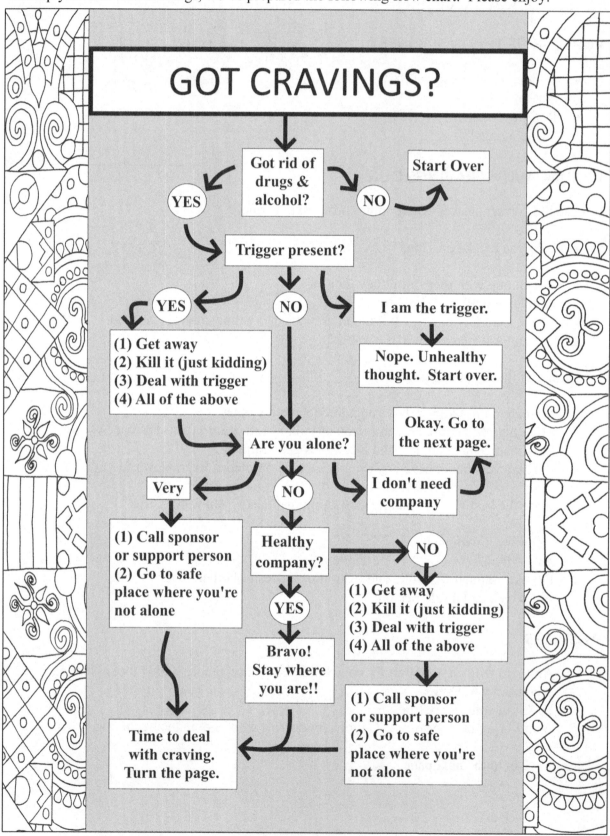

BACK TO WAYS TO DEAL WITH CRAVINGS

There are *many* Urge-Management Mind-Mesmerizing Methods (UMMMM), or strategies for dealing with cravings. Below you'll find two.

1. The Pause and Distract UMMMM

Cravings come and go. The trick is to distract yourself until the craving is gone. Follow these instructions.

   a. Set a timer for 60 minutes. Promise yourself not to use during that time period.
   b. Distract yourself. Do something that has nothing to do with addiction. Preferably something healthy. No, definitely something healthy.
   c. If the craving is still present after 60 minutes, repeat the process. Extend to 24 hours, as tolerated.

In the box on the right, describe 10 activities you can use to distract yourself.

2. The Urge Surfing UMMMM

With urge surfing, you stay with the urge until it loses its power. How do you urge surf? Here's how: Look inward at the urge and, using the space below, answer the following questions using *one long sentence*.

Where is the craving? What does it look like? What sensations are you experiencing? What are you feeling and thinking? Watch the craving and describe it disappearing little by little. Stay with it until it doesn't matter so much.

Remember, one long sentence.

Distract Away

List ten activities to distract yourself when you have cravings.

_____
_____
_____
_____
_____
_____
_____
_____
_____
_____

Can't come up with enough distractions? Here's our list. Check those that might work.

"Fun" distractions

☐ Call a (healthy) friend
☐ Listen to music
☐ Watch a funny movie
☐ Get a massage
☐ Play with a pet
☐ Window-shop on Amazon
☐ Ride a motorcycle
☐ Go bungie jumping

Other distractions

☐ Pay bills
☐ Clean the house
☐ Go for a walk
☐ Relax all your muscles
☐ Practice mindfulness
☐ Write in a journal
☐ Call sponsor or mentor
☐ Go to a 12-step meeting
☐ Read OTB Recovery

REFLECTION

The next time you feel like using, call it "Episode #1" and practice the listed UMMMM. Answer the questions in the box. Repeat for Episode #2.

Craving episode #1:

How intense was the craving at the beginning? _____

Which UMMMM did you use?   DISTRACTION

How did you distract yourself? How many times did you need to repeat before it helped?
_____
_____

How intense was the craving after the UMMMM? _____

Craving episode #2:

How intense was the craving at the beginning? _____

Which UMMMM did you use?   URGE SURFING

Grab a piece of paper and write one long sentence describing the urge. Where is it? What does it look like? Describe all associated sensations, feelings, thoughts.

What was this like UMMMM like for you? _____

How intense was the craving after the UMMMM? _____

Great! Move onto Day 12 (page 41) to learn more UMMMMMMMMM's.

DAY 12. GETTING PAST CRAVINGS II

PURPOSE OF THIS WORKSHEET:

- To identify more ways to get past cravings

MORE URGE-BUSTING STRATEGIES

In the last worksheet, we discussed two ways to deal with cravings. To reveal a longer list, please unscramble the words below and plug each word into the crossword puzzle.

ACROSS	DOWN
4. _____ (AKTL) to a therapist, mentor, wise friend, sponsor, or someone you trust. 6. Go to a 12-step _____ (ETEIMGN). 8. _____ (VIADO) the trigger. 9. Read your _____ (LAESPRE) Prevention Plan. 10. _____ (PTOS) the thought. Say NO. 11. _____ (RIEEVW) your reasons to quit. 12. Do sports or _____ (XERECSIE).	1. Don't be _____ (NLAOE). Spend time with sober and clean people. 2. _____ (TARSIDCT) yourself. Get busy and do something! 3. Use _____ (PCNOGI) skills. 4. Identify the _____ (RGRTIGE). 5. Deal with the _____ (BORPMEL). 6. _____ (IDTMTEEA) or be mindful. 7. Remember, the _____ (VINRACG) goes away on its own. Just wait it out.

(See Appendix C for answers)

YOUR TURN

Between this and the previous worksheet (Day 11), we've described dozens of ways to deal with cravings. On Day 11, you described 2 craving episodes. Pay attention to new cravings that come up today; choose 2 more methods and describe what happens.

Consider sharing your results with a counselor, sponsor, or friend.

Craving Episode #3

Method you used to deal with craving: _____

Describe what you did:

The intensity of craving before method: _____

The intensity of craving after method: _____

Length of craving _____

Craving Episode #4

Method you used to deal with craving: _____

Describe what you did:

The intensity of craving before method: _____

The intensity of craving after method: _____

Length of craving _____

OH DEAR, A QUIZ.

Alright, to pull things together, here's a quick true/false quiz.

1. True   False   As a person with addiction, you'll always have cravings.
2. True   False   The best way to avoid relapse is to have a relapse prevention plan.
3. True   False   People can always tell what it is that's triggering a craving.
4. True   False   Hanging out with using friends can be a trigger.
5. True   False   The best way to stay clean is to be strong and decide not to use.

ANSWERS TO TRUE/FALSE QUESTIONS

1. Answers will vary, but typically this is false. Most often, cravings subside over time.
2. True.
3. False. Often it's not obvious. Triggers like scents, memories, sounds, thoughts, or sensations (hunger, pain, exhaustion) can affect you without your knowing it.
4. True.
5. False. You shouldn't rely on strength and will-power to overcome drugs, especially in the beginning. It's better to avoid triggers altogether and get into the habit of saying NO without thinking.

REFLECTION

For you personally, what are the best ways to deal with cravings and triggers?

Not sure? We have a list! Check all options that might work for you.

Deal with Craving

- ☐ *Distract yourself.*
- ☐ *Use Urge Surfing.*
- ☐ *Exercise.*
- ☐ *Don't be alone.*
- ☐ *Meditate. Practice mindfulness.*
- ☐ *Learn new ways to deal with stress.*
- ☐ *Talk to someone you trust.*
- ☐ *Go to a 12-step meeting.*
- ☐ *Spend time with "safe" people.*
- ☐ *Stop the thought. Say NO.*

Deal with Trigger

- ☐ *Avoid trigger.*
- ☐ *Get away from trigger.*
- ☐ *Get rid of trigger (when applicable).*
- ☐ *Change trigger in a good way.*
- ☐ *Change your reaction to trigger.*
- ☐ *Change how you think about trigger.*
- ☐ *Ask a friend for help.*
- ☐ *Plan ahead how to deal with trigger.*
- ☐ *Review reasons you want to quit.*
- ☐ *Think about consequences of relapsing.*

This worksheet is over, but dealing with cravings isn't. Make sure to use these strategies often!

The Outside-the-Box Recovery Workbook

PLEASE
TAKE A BREAK

Before moving on, can you find your way through this recovery maze, from start to finish? It's a child's task, yes, but have fun anyway. Please see Appendix C for the answer.

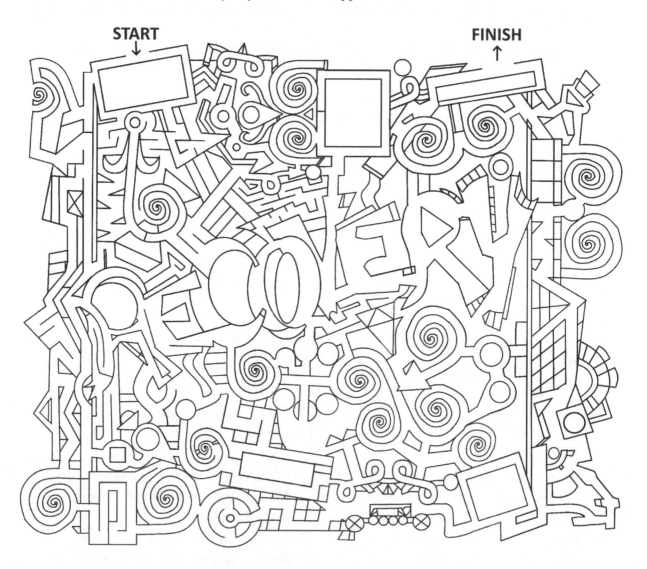

DAY 13. GRIEVING THE LOSS OF ADDICTION I

PURPOSE OF THIS WORKSHEET:

- To recognize it's okay to miss the past
- To find ways to let the past go and focus on recovery

You have lots of questions: How do you survive life without drugs and alcohol? Will you ever feel good again? Is sobriety worth the effort? Is recovery even possible? No worries. You got this. Here's a worksheet to get you going.

THE COMPLAINT

First, let's figure out what you're dealing with. Answer the questions below. This is your space, a safe place to say what you're really feeling.

a. What are the "benefits" of addiction?

b. What do you miss about using and drinking?

c. What don't you like about recovery?

THE COUNTER-ARGUMENT

As much as you miss drugs and alcohol, addiction messed you up. But how? You've answered these questions before, maybe hundreds of times, but it's important to write your answers again.

a. What don't you like about addiction?

b. What's good about recovery?

c. What does sobriety give you that using or drinking can't?

d. Why choose recovery over addiction?

FINDING CLOSURE

Imagine you've just left a stunningly gorgeous but *abusive* lover. This is the fifth time you've tried to get away. Now you're sitting in a third-rate hotel room in the bad part of town. You've been sitting on the bed studying the bedcover design for the past hour.

You're lonely. You're depressed. To make things worse, your ex-lover keeps texting. They promise to change. "Please come back," they say. "I'm worried about you."

You want to go home. But you know the truth. You can't have a healthy relationship with this person. That is, you can't have a healthy relationship with addiction. What do you do? You need to say goodbye. We suggest you start with a pen and go to the next page!

The Outside-the-Box Recovery Workbook

INSTRUCTIONS:

Write a letter breaking it off with addiction. This may sound ridiculous, but it grants insight, gives you context and finality, and makes room for closure. Use the space below.

REFLECTION

What did you learn about yourself and your relationship with drugs/alcohol in this exercise? How did it help you say goodbye to addiction?

You've written a letter. That's an enormous step, but it's just a start. You'll need to symbolically, purposefully, obsessively, emphatically say goodbye to addiction – over and over. There are a million ways to do this. Writing a letter is one. The next worksheet (page 48) takes on a few more ways to end a relationship with addiction.

DAY 14. GRIEVING THE LOSS OF ADDICTION II

PURPOSE OF THIS WORKSHEET:

- To find ways to let the past go and focus on recovery

As a person in recovery, it's impossible to have a healthy relationship with drugs and alcohol – but addiction follows you around anyway, and sometimes it seems more attractive than quitting and staying quit. How do you deal with that? We recommend you practice saying goodbye to chemical dependency repeatedly until it isn't as overpowering as before. But don't lose focus. This isn't about addiction. This is about recovery and establishing a life worth living!

WAYS TO LET THE PAST GO.

Below we list several ways to say goodbye to addiction and hello to recovery. Pick a method and do it, then answer the reflection questions on the next page.

WORDS AND PICTURES

→ *Goodbye.* Collect images that symbolize addiction: photographs, drawings, printed images, anything. Look them over one at a time. For each, say "*I want addiction out of my life because…*" and finish the sentence. When you've said what needs to be said, bid farewell to that part of your life by tearing the pictures into pieces and tossing them away.

→ *Hello.* Find pictures that symbolizes your future in recovery. Put them in a folder marked "recovery" and each day add something new. Review frequently.

ROCKS IN THE RIVER

→ *Goodbye.* Think of words that represent addiction. They can be a person, place, thought, feeling, etc. When ready, collect a bunch of large stones. Use a marker to write one word on each stone. Next, place the stones in a stream or toss them into a river or lake. For each stone, say "*I want addiction out of my life because…*" and finish the sentence.

→ *Hello.* Find some flowers: real, fake, doodled, or printed off the internet. Put them somewhere in view. These represent recovery. Replace them every few days.

JOURNAL THE PAIN, JOURNAL THE FUTURE

→ *Goodbye.* Grab a pen and notebook and write about addiction, the goods and the bads. Take as long as you need. When finished, cross it all out and, in large and prominent letters write "*I want addiction out of my life because…*" and complete the sentence.

→ *Hello.* Write about the person you wish to be and how recovery helps point you in the right direction. This is about your future, so take your time!

REFLECTION

As attractive as substance abuse can be, it's never a healthy partner. Farewell rituals help break that link between chemical dependency and you. Hopefully you completed one of the tasks from today's options. If not, go back and do it now! Next, complete the following:

Which ritual did you choose?

_____

How much time did you spend doing it?

_____

What was toxic about your connection with drugs or alcohol? Why end the relationship?

How did the ritual help?

How will you know when addiction no longer has a hold on you? (Tough question!)

Remember that saying goodbye to addiction is NOT as important as saying hello to recovery. Don't stay with the grief. Find joy in a future without drugs. How do you do that? What can you do to make things better? On page 50, we start working on these questions.

DAY 15. GRIEVING THE LOSS OF ADDICTION III

PURPOSE OF THIS WORKSHEET:

- To let the past go
- To focus on recovery
- To replace addiction with something worthwhile

Recovery points you toward the *future*, and that's a worthwhile place to be – if you choose to make it so. But how do you choose your future? Today we take a small step in that direction. We write a wish list.

THE WISH LIST

A wish list is a string of written hopes and dreams. It serves many purposes.

- A wish list helps you identify your "true north." Want to know where you'd like to be in five, ten, or fifty years? Write a wish list.

- A wish list cheers you up. There's a little part of you that needs to dream, regardless of reality's limitations, and here's your chance to do so. Want to win the lottery? Hope to ride a white dragon some day? Write a wish list.

- A wish list makes your dreams more likely to happen. Call it attitude, belief system, self-fulfilling prophecy, magic, Higher Power, or a kind universe – things tend to fall into place when you write a wish list....

Suspend doubt and give it a try. Either you write and nothing happens, or the universe (or you) gets busy. What do you have to lose? Using the space on the right, write your darned list.

INSTRUCTIONS

Write your wishes for each of the categories below.

a. Recovery

b. Passion/Spiritual

c. Health

d. Possessions

e. Friendship

f. Romance

g. Career/education

h. Other

You've started a list of dreams. Reaching these dreams, replacing addiction with something worthwhile, doesn't happen overnight. Be patient. Stay tuned.

REFLECTION

How did you feel about the future before writing your wish list?

How do you feel about your future now? How did your point of view change?

What can you do to make it okay to hope and dream more?

How likely is it that the stuff on your list will come true?

(We revisit this list on Day 29 (page 89). Stay tuned!)

SOLVE THIS CODE PLEASE

Welcome. Relax a moment. Meanwhile, can you decipher this cipher?

SOLVE CODE PLEASE.
Do you agree with this quotation? Why or why not?

PROBLEMS PROBLEMS
PROBLEMS PROBLEMS
PROBLEMS PROBLEMS

A	B	C	D	E	F	G	H	I	J	K	L	M
巳	兀	ヨ	二	月	氺	四	艹	阝	青	卤	宀	示
N	O	P	Q	R	S	T	U	V	W	X	Y	Z
犬	田	白	网	艸	血	谷	龠	毛	方	彡	广	干

PROBLEMS PROBLEMS PROBLEMS ARGH PROBLEMS
"I've realized that instead of posting all my problems on Facebook, it's better to find solutions for them on Google." - B Franco

(See Appendix C for answers.)

DAY 16. INTRODUCING CHANGE

PURPOSE OF THIS WORKSHEET:

- To introduce the importance of change in recovery

CHANGE

Imagine you've been using or drinking for years but suddenly wake up determined to quit. *Yep, time to quit.* All drugs and alcohol are thrown out. You do the rehab thing then head back home.

1. You're clean now. That's all that matters. You make no changes in your lifestyle. You hang out with the same using friends at the same using hangouts. How likely is it you'll stay clean and sober? (Choose more than one)

   a. Naw, man, back to drugs within a week.
   b. You'll stay clean and sober for three hours.
   c. You won't be sober for long, not even three hours.
   d. One way or another, you'll likely relapse – and fast.

   You've guessed it by now. Getting over chemical dependency and changing lifestyle go hand-in-hand. Want to change one? You have to change the other. (Any or all of the options are correct.)

2. You've relapsed. Right now, a typical day involves a cup of coffee, six beers, a morning on the couch watching reruns on TV, brushing your teeth left to right, six more drinks, a long nap, then a walk to the store at 5 p.m. for cigarettes and more beer. You plan to quit and make changes. Which of the following counts as change? (Choose one or more)

   a. A walk in the morning to a coffee shop → cup of coffee → brush your teeth right to left → watch a documentary on TV at your (sober) brother's house.
   b. Brush your teeth top to bottom → watch the news for an hour → drink a cup of coffee → invite your (sober) brother for a walk.
   c. Move to sober living → get a job → go to meetings every day → save the world.
   d. Drink a cup of coffee → *brush* four beers → *drink* the TV → *watch* your toothbrush → *drink* a nap → *take* more beer → walk to store for beer and a cigarette.

   And the answer? Sure, the third one is the best choice. Who doesn't want to save the world? But A and B are perfectly respectable: you're changing your schedule, avoiding triggers, and spending time with sober people. All answers are good except the last one, which makes no sense. We're not even sure why it's there. Please move onto the exercise on the next page.

PRACTICE CHANGE RIGHT HERE, RIGHT NOW.

Choose a song or story and jot it down in the box below marked "original." Use the other box to rewrite the story or give it a different ending.

Here's an example:

Before: Mary had a little lamb whose fleece was as white as snow, and everywhere that Mary went the lamb was sure to go.

After: Mary had a little snake whose bite was sure to Mary break, and everywhere that Mary ran that damned lil snake kept her awake.

Original	Rewrite

Embrace Change

REFLECTION

How hard was it to change the lyrics?

How hard is it to change in real life?

Right now, what changes are you working on in your life? List the top five here.

Change #1
Change #2
Change #3
Change #4
Change #5

We'll talk more about change in the next worksheet on page 56.

DAY 17. CHANGE WHAT YOU DO

NO MATTER WHERE MARGARET WENT, CHANGE ALWAYS FOLLOWED.

PURPOSE OF THIS WORKSHEET:

- To identify changes that promote recovery
- To balance self-acceptance and change

QUIT = LIVE HAPPILY EVER AFTER?

After years of cocaine abuse, jail sentences, and rehabs, you've been clean for 12 months. While you don't consider yourself an expert, you've got a friend who just quit using yesterday, and he's asked you for advice. "I quit," he says. "I'm never going to use again."

1. Your friend is from the "**Quit = Live Happily Ever After**" school of thinking. You mention something about lifestyle change. He looks at you with skepticism. "Change, really? Why do I need to change?" It's a good question. Why change? Why not stick with the familiar? Write your answer below.

2. It's 6 hours later. By now you've convinced your friend change is necessary. He's ready to adjust his life completely. He pauses thoughtfully. "But what do I need to change?" Describe two changes that are necessary for successful recovery.

change change change change change change change change change change change change change

3. Despite his enthusiasm, your friend is frazzled. Change is difficult. What advice would you give to calm him down?
   a. "Take it one day at a time."
   b. "Change what needs to be changed."
   c. "Accept what you can't change."
   d. All of the above.
   e. Yep, all of the above.

ANSWERS

1. Addiction likes to be number one in your life, the beginning and the end and everything in between. Chemicals are often the only enjoyment and skill and friend a person has when they're using. Quitting means rewriting life's narrative. How do you have fun without using? How do you cope with panic and not drink? How do you battle isolation when everyone you know is an addict? In recovery, drugs aren't the answer. Your only option is change.
2. Answers will vary. Changes usually involve friendship, environment, choices, reactions to triggers, healthy avoidance, and sometimes living situation. We'll touch more on this in the next 3 worksheets (pages 59-66).
3. Yeah, yeah, all of the above.

BALANCING ACCEPTANCE AND CHANGE

Change is everywhere, but sometimes changes are *not* good. In fact, some are impossible. Alas, recovery means telling the difference between what you can and can't change.

Below you'll find a list of problems and choices. Circle all that are NOT helpful for recovery or those that CANNOT be changed.

   a. Increasing social support, like 12-step meetings or a SMART program.
   b. Buying a gun illegally to take care of a neighborhood problem.
   c. Blackmailing people who don't support you and your recovery.
   d. Getting a job as a bartender or bouncer in a club.
   e. Identifying triggers and avoiding them; if they can't be avoided, adjusting to them.
   f. Approaching problems with a new perspective or point of view.
   g. Your sister walking on eggshells to avoid upsetting you.
   h. Being so tall you bump your head on the ceiling everywhere you go.

change change change change change change change change change change change change change

i. Not bending the rules or looking for loopholes.
j. Confronting all your demons right away.
k. Feeling miserable about cheating on your spouse ten years ago
l. Deciding to be honest about a mistake you made.

ANSWERS

Choices that are bad for recovery or can't be changed include B, C, D, G, H, K, and possibly J. H doesn't jeopardize recovery, but it's a characteristic you can't change. K is a past action that can't be undone. G is an example of co-dependency or enabling. Most people would agree J isn't a good idea, especially in early recovery, but opinions will vary.

HOMEWORK

We don't give homework often, but here's a tiny task: Do something usual in a different way. It doesn't have to be big, but step outside your comfort zone. Check one of the following ideas and give it a try.

- ☐ Brush your teeth with your nondominant hand
- ☐ Shower doing your washing routine backwards
- ☐ Drink from a glass using your nondominant hand
- ☐ Instead of smoking right after coffee, chew on a toothpick for 20 minutes
- ☐ Don't look at your cellphone for a full hour
- ☐ Write a few sentences with your nondominant hand
- ☐ Text someone using your nondominant hand

REFLECTION

We asked you to do something in a different way. How did the change feel? Why?

DAY 18. CHANGE HOW YOU TALK

PURPOSE OF THIS WORKSHEET:

- To explore how spoken words affect recovery
- To identify and avoid addiction war talk

IMAGINE YOU'RE AT AN AA MEETING. "Judy" is talking about her experience as an addict. "Let me tell you the funniest story. Once I was trying to light [A], getting high on [B], when [C] caught on fire, and I tried [D] and [E] before calling [F]!" "Fred" pipes up, his smile so wide it's contagious. "I always wondered what would happen if you mixed [A-F] together." Judy chuckles. "Christ, I miss those [A-F] days…"

1. START HERE. Why is this a troubling scenario?
   a. Because we're revealing the names of people attending an AA meeting.
   b. Because they're laughing and having fun, which is forbidden.
   c. Because they're downplaying the seriousness of using and drinking.

2. What are addiction war stories? Why are they a problem?

3. What's the difference between war stories and healthy talk about substance use disorders?

Next page

6. Which of the following are war stories?
   a. Talking about unusual ways to use heroin.
   b. Obsessive discussion about controlled prescription drugs, including how they work, appearance and doctors who prescribe them.
   c. Preparing to ask your doctor for an amphetamine for attention problems but respecting their answer if they say NO.
   d. Describing the death of a friend from overdose the night you were using together.

5. What's the best way to deal with war stories? Cross out all options that aren't helpful.
   a. Stop talking and change the subject.
   b. Hell, war stories can be hilarious. People need the comic relief. Just let people talk.
   c. It's important to speak about addiction, but the conversation must promote recovery.
   d. Finish the war story then apologize or say, "Just kidding."
   e. If the conversation becomes a trigger, get away and distract yourself.

4. Seriously: Why not glamorize drugs?

ANSWERS

1. C. The speakers are glorifying the "good old days." They're glamorizing addiction. These tales are called *war stories*, and they stand in the way of recovery.

2-4. War stories include any drug-related communication that gets in the way of recovery, like pro-drug jokes, glorification of chemical dependency, or unhealthy fascination with certain medications. War stories are often a sign that someone isn't ready to quit. They can also destabilize others who are still on the fence. Healthy discussion about addiction supports sobriety.

5. B and D aren't good ways to deal with war stories.

6. A and B are war stories.

REFLECTION

What kinds of drug-related stories are okay to share?

What about jokes? How can you tell if a joke is good for recovery?

In the end, Judy and Fred's comments undermine the seriousness of the meeting and do little to point others in the direction of recovery. If everyone laughs and agrees, it sets a standard that drugs are sometimes acceptable. In recovery, there's no room for "drugs are sometimes acceptable!"

DAY 19. CHANGE AND ALTER EGO I

PURPOSE OF THIS WORKSHEET:

- To enable change by considering how you want to grow

CREATING AN ALTER EGO is an unusual way to better understand your ideal self. It can also help identify new ways to approach your problems. Up for the challenge? Use this handout to create an AE.

IMAGINE yourself as what you'd like to be in the future. That's your Alter Ego (AE). Use this worksheet to explore what ideal *recovery* looks like, whether fantasy or reality-based.

Apart from being in recovery, what is your AE like? Not sure? See below and the next page for ideas. Circle the characteristics that sound right, then fill out the chart at the end of today's worksheet.

APPEARANCE

Looks like you	Opposite to you	Muscular/fit	Gorgeous
Colorful	Survival scars	Elderly	Wise-looking
Pitch black hair	Sunglasses	Wears cape	Childlike

PERSONALITY

Happy	Eccentric	Artistic	Very creative
Giving	Honest	Heroic	Humble
Intelligent	Funny	Outgoing	Reflective

Alter Ego

Circle the characteristics that appeal to you.

EXPERIENCES (GOOD AND BAD)

Married	Has children	Divorced	Single
Widowed	Very educated	Criminal past	Made mistakes
Has secrets	Was homeless	Good job	Orphan
Overcame a lot	Survived abuse	Works hard	World-traveler

ACTIONS

Draws/paints	Plays instrument	Writes	Dances
Helps others	Studies a lot	Races cars	Calms dragons
Makes money	Lucky in love	Knows tech	Raises kids

REPUTATION

Misunderstood	Survivor	Fair and kind	Mysterious
Has integrity	Worthy	Lively	Appreciated
Admirable	Wise	Jokester	Brilliant

WHAT RECOVERY IS LIKE

Challenging	Worthwhile	Rewarding	Did it alone
Whew, tough	Self-accepting	12-step	Very satisfying

The Outside-the-Box Recovery Workbook

Below you'll find a "Chart of Desired Traits."
Fill in each box, referring to the ideas you've
circled so far and adding your own.

CHART OF DESIRED TRAITS
(What's your AE like?)

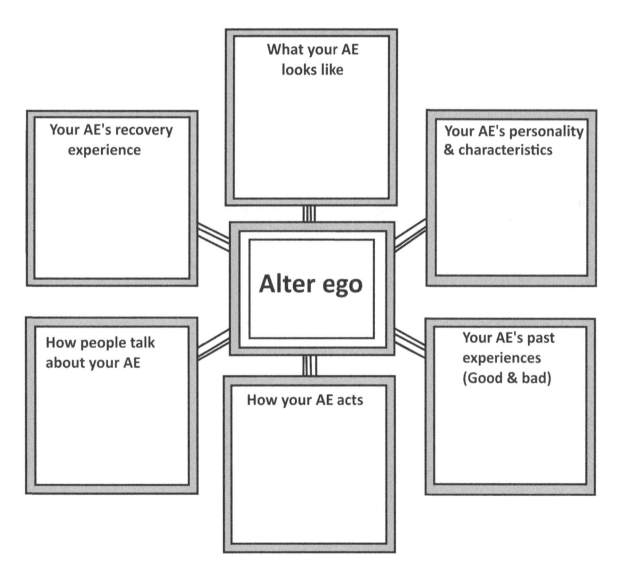

A great start. Move onto Day 20 (page 64), and we'll take it to the next level!

63

DAY 20. CHANGE AND ALTER EGO II

PURPOSE OF THIS WORKSHEET:

- To temporarily "step outside yourself" and see things differently
- To learn more about your ideal self

Scenario 1. Your alter ego (AE) has made the same mistakes you made. Describe one major mistake from the past.

START HERE. Your alter ego is who you want to be someday. To better understand this person, consider what they would do in the following circumstances.

Your AE deals with the mistake in a healthy way and finds peace. How do they do that? They…

a. Understand they did the best they could with what they knew at the time
b. Help others or volunteer
c. Feel proud for having become a better person
d. Decide to never repeat the mistake
e. Your idea:

Scenario 2. Your ideal self just started a new job. They love the job, except for a coworker who falsely gossips that your AE is "still using." Everyone believes them. How does your AE react? What do they do?

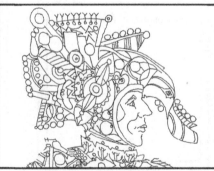

The Outside-the-Box Recovery Workbook

Alter Ego

Scenario 3. What is your AE's life like? Where would they live? What would they do during the day? Write your answer in the column to the right.

Describe your AE's life (your ideal future) here:

How is your life different to your AE's?

Apart from staying clean, describe one thing you can do to point yourself towards your ideal life.

ANSWERS

Scenario One. Mistakes can haunt you, but there are ways to right past wrongs. We'll talk more about dealing with regrets on Days 22-25 (pages 69-80).

Scenario Two. People don't always recognize that you've changed, nor do they recognize the tremendous effort recovery takes. You'll need time to earn back trust. Expect it to happen little by little. Stick at it and don't let others misdirect your recovery. We talk more about this on Days 24 and 25 (pages 76-80).

Scenario Three. This scenario is about your goals. Defining what you want out of life gives you direction. Refer to Days 15 (page 50) and 29 (page 89) for more information.

REFLECTION

1. Why create an AE? In the list below, circle all that are good reasons to create an AE.

- a. To establish where you want to go and how to get there
- b. To give you an excuse to do bad things
- c. To forget who you really are
- d. To explore alternative perspectives
- e. To have a different side of your personality "step in" and help during difficult situations
- f. To lend more depth to your personal story
- g. To replace reality with a dreamworld
- h. Because AEs are always superheroes.

The benefits of creating an AE include A, D, E, and F. The others are all false. An AE can help you see yourself, life, and future from a different point of view, give you strength in tough situations, and give you extra help during challenging moments.

2. What did you learn about yourself in this worksheet?

PLEASE SOLVE THIS PUZZLE

This workbook is about recovery. That also means sobriety.
How many times can you find the word SOBER in this word search puzzle?

SOBER

R	S	R	O	R	E	B	O	S	B
E	O	R	E	B	O	S	O	R	E
B	E	R	S	S	O	B	E	R	S
O	S	E	R	R	E	B	O	S	O
S	O	B	E	R	O	S	O	R	B
E	B	O	B	S	O	B	E	R	E
R	E	S	O	R	E	B	O	S	R
S	R	B	S	R	S	O	B	E	R

(See Appendix C for answers.)

DAY 21. ADDICTION'S EFFECT ON OTHERS

PURPOSE OF THIS WORKSHEET:

- To recognize the effect addiction has on others
- To devote a moment to those you've hurt

CHEMICAL DEPENDENCY HURTS EVERYONE. Who have you wounded or offended because of addiction? Below, draw a face or stick figure for each person. As you sketch the individual, consider their feelings. Consider the consequences they suffered, what they felt like, and how they're affected even now.

Give each individual at least 5 minutes before moving onto the next.

REFLECTION

Did you include a stick-figure drawing of yourself? If not, make sure to add YOU.

DAY 22. THE INTERVIEW: RECOGNIZING MISTAKES

PURPOSE OF THIS WORKSHEET:

- To examine how addiction affected your behaviors in the past
- To recognize regret and heartache

IMAGINE YOU'RE THE MOST POPULAR TALK SHOW HOST ON TV. You're known for your no-nonsense, nasty interview style.

Today you're interviewing a mystery guest hiding behind Curtain #1. The camera goes live. You read the prompt. *"The person behind the curtain has a painful, pathetic past. They're here to tell us about life as an addict. They're here to confess the mistake they've made."* You pause. The public loves this kind of stuff. *"Mystery Guest, please step into view and join me on stage."*

A feeble old person steps out and hobbles up to the chair beside you. Their skin is littered with crevices, fold upon fold of wrinkly, velvety skin. The individual shoots a kind smile at you, too kind for your taste – but immediately you know why. *They are YOU.*

REALLY TOUGH QUESTIONS

As a TV host, you have a list of pre-planned questions. On the next page you'll find a share of them. Looking honestly at your past mistakes, answer all questions openly and in writing – as the addict, not TV host. No worries, this isn't going on real TV!

Describe three major mistakes you made in the past. Using the space below and on the next page, start at the beginning and explain what happened. For each mistake, answer the following questions.

- What happened? Why?
- How did the mistake affect others?
- How did it affect you?

- Has it happened again?
- How does it affect others now?
- How does it affect you now?

Mistake #1.

Mistake #2.

Mistake #3.

REFLECTION

The interview ends. The audience is silent as you leave the stage. Why is the audience quiet? Out of surprise, empathy, sadness, hostility?

Why is it important to understand and process past mistakes? (If you're not sure, search online for more information and write your findings below.)

This was a hard worksheet. On Day 23 (page 72), we start making sense out of the interview.

DAY 23. AFTER THE INTERVIEW: MISTAKES & HOPE

PURPOSE OF THIS WORKSHEET:

- To reflect on ways to make up for past mistakes
- To encourage pride in right decisions and growth

(This is a continuation from Day 22, pages 69-71, "The Interview: Recognizing Mistakes." If you haven't completed it already, please do so now!)

YOU'VE BEEN IN RECOVERY 60 YEARS and were interviewed about it on TV. The experience was horrible. The TV host was nasty. Instead of celebrating recovery, you confessed to miserable things.

As a person who's overcome chemical dependency and been sober all these years, you don't wallow in shame. Instead, you write a "Letter to the Editor" in your local newspaper to deal with the past and remember what you did right. You might be 93 years old, but you've got attitude!

INSTRUCTIONS:

It took strength to quit. It takes strength to stay in recovery. Use that strength to take on past mistakes. Mistakes include character flaws, resentment, destructive behaviors, etc.

You're going to write a letter to "publicly" list and deal with these issues. Choose three past mistakes (ideally the ones you wrote about on Day 22), and use the template on the next 2 pages to describe how you improved or plan to improve the situation for each one. Be specific. Address the letter to "Dear Editor." Consider using the following phrases:

I improved/improve myself by...

I healed/heal those I hurt by...

Things I do/can do to make a difference include...

If you haven't "righted the wrong" yet, write about what you will do. Again, be specific!

The Outside-the-Box Recovery Workbook

Central Times

Limited Edition Limited Edition Limited Edition Limited Edition Limited

How drugs hijacked my LIFE
AND WHAT I DID ABOUT IT

Not sure how to make up for past mistakes? Here are some ideas.

- Apologize with *actions*.
- Make it up to the person you hurt, even in small ways.
- If you can't make amends with the person you wronged, help others by volunteering or doing good.
- Don't repeat the mistake.
- Plan what you can do differently next time you're in that situation.

WRITE A LETTER FOR THE NEWSPAPER describing three past mistakes and how you improved/can improve the situation for each one.

(Continue on the next page)

"I always find heroes who are just like me, I forget they're only human, and like me, broken."
Terrence Alonzo Craft, The Seed Bridge: Collected Poems

Central Times

Limited Edition Limited Edition Limited Edition Limited Edition Limited

(Continued)

HOW my mistakes made me a BETTER person

REFLECTION

Review your letter. By now you've described many things you can do to make up for past wrongs. But sometimes no matter what you do, you can't make it up to the person you hurt. What then?

Not sure? We take on tough mistakes on Days 24-25 (pages 76-80). Stay tuned.

Take a break
PLEASE

TIPS FOR RECOVERY. Apart from attending 12-Step meetings, there are dozens of actions that promote recovery. Please try out the following tips – and find them in the word search below. See Appendix C for answers.

- Get support
- Practice honesty
- Improve skills
- Don't rely on will power
- Understand relapse
- See self as non-user
- No negative thinking
- Be honorable
- Avoid triggers
- Care for self
- Avoid using friends
- Deal with cravings
- Change habits
- Have fun sober
- Don't bend rules
- Say no
- Stay clean and sober
- Be open to change

```
A B S T A Y C L E A N A N D S O B E R C
V R H A N T H H D A R R B T U U G G A E
O S E E S E L F A S N O N U S E R R D G
I S E W O T C F D N D E G G T W E R O N
D U R F O D R G I B G D E S I F T D E A
U A B N G P E L D N A E U E O T H F S H
S D E F F N L N U K D P H R Y H Y D E C
I R H D M D T L H Y P H S A Y N O U L O
N E O T A N L B I O N E O U B Y T U U T
G B N D K G H F R W L E G B D I B Y R N
F O O R E C B T A F N N V N B D T T D E
R S R E G G I R T D I O V A N I S S N P
I N A N O G E C G H A C Y U L J E O E O
E U B D A R B R H A E G N L E B H S B E
N F L T L A E N J O Y L I F E J R Z T B
D E E E S P A L E R D N A T S R E D N U
S V S I M P R O V E S K I L L S T A O N
R A D E A L W I T H C R A V I N G D G
G H G N I K N I H T E V I T A G E N O N
P R A C T I C E H O N E S T Y J B H E D
```

DAY 24. MISTAKES WITHOUT FORGIVENESS

PURPOSE OF THIS WORKSHEET:

- To further explore ways to deal with mistakes and guilt, especially unresolved issues

IMAGINE YOU'RE IN REHAB.

You're a 17-year-old girl hooked on heroin who just checked herself into a long-term rehab.

Over the past few years, you've stolen your uncle's credit card, totaled his car, withdrawn 6000 dollars from his bank account, and done a list of other things you're not proud of.

1. What are the worst ways to deal with past regrets? Circle all UNHEALTHY options.

a. Repeat the same mistake again.	j. Once possible, pay your uncle back 10 dollars/month.
b. Clean up your uncle's yard every Sunday and help cut grass.	k. Volunteer at the local shelter helping addicts.
c. Feel paralyzed and do nothing.	l. Teach teenagers skills to avoid drugs.
d. Avoid repeating the mistake.	m. Keep using drugs to avoid thinking about bad things you've done.
e. Get angry at your uncle for making you feel guilty.	n. Buy yourself a therapy dog.
f. Act like it never happened.	o. Punish yourself severely for what you did.
g. Beat somebody up for the fun of it.	p. Think your uncle has lots of money, so it shouldn't matter.
h. Ask for forgiveness.	q. Work on building integrity.
i. Stay in treatment.	r. Not change a thing

Reactions to AVOID include A, C, E, F, G, M, O, P, R. N might be helpful or problematic, depending on your living situation, allergies, and how much you like to get slobbered.

2. What is the best way to deal with mistakes when you're in early recovery?

   a. Stay clean
   b. Stay away from drugs and alcohol
   c. Remain in recovery
   d. Don't relapse

e. All of the above
f. E
g. None of the above
h. Just kidding, G is wrong

You've guessed it: all except G are correct. Dealing with regrets begins with recovery. Without staying clean and sober, nothing else matters.

10 YEARS LATER: FAMILY REUNION

Now you're a 27-year-old recovered heroin addict.

Tonight is the big family reunion. You're nervous, but there's also pride and integrity in your step. You haven't seen your family since you quit. Your husband reassures you. *Everything is going to be okay. You're a different person.*

With your husband and pig-tailed daughter at your side, you step into the hallway where the family awaits. Your uncle sees you. He forces a grin. He isn't happy. "Stay away from my credit card and car," he says.

3. How can you make things better with your uncle?

4. What if he won't forgive you?

The rest of the night is a disaster. You'd hoped for kindness, even acceptance, but most of your family avoid you. Those who don't are unfriendly. Everyone remembers you as you were, not as you are. *Come*, says a familiar voice, *it's time to go home.* Your husband hooks his arm around yours. He leads you outside to get some air. Your daughter bounces along beside you.

5. You realize that no matter what you do, your family won't forgive you. How do you deal with your family's rejection?

REFLECTION

Sometimes no matter what you do right, things still turn out wrong. Think of a time you hurt someone who wouldn't forgive you, no matter what you did. Describe the situation here.

What can you do to right this wrong?

Need ideas? Here's a list of ways to right unforgiveable wrongs.

- *Stay in recovery.*
- *If helpful, let the person know you'll be waiting if or when they're ready to talk. Then let them go.*
- *Write the person a letter describing the changes you're making, how you're working towards doing things differently. Focus on changing actions, not apologizing with words. DON'T send the letter, but DO do what you say you're going to do.*
- *If you can't make life better for the person you injured, make life better for someone else. Do this often.*
- *Secretly do something caring in the person's honor, like volunteer or pay for a stranger's meal or donate money to a cause. Do this often.*
- *Secretly do something meaningful or symbolic in their honor, like pray or write poetry. Do this often.*
- *Forgive people who hurt you.*
- *Be a better person.*
- *Don't repeat the mistake.*

DAY 25. SELF-FORGIVENESS

PURPOSE OF THIS WORKSHEET:

- To forgive yourself and create a blank slate
- To also take responsibility for your actions

WRITE YOURSELF A LETTER.

Please write a letter forgiving yourself sincerely and completely for past mistakes. Use the space on the right.

Make sure to take responsibility for what you did, promise to not repeat it, and allow yourself the chance to start with a fresh slate.

Remember: This is about forgiveness, not forgetting!

REFLECTION

What is it like to truly forgive yourself? Rather than exploring this question with words, first do something odd: reflect on your answer while shading in or coloring the pictures below. For the first, draw your feelings before self-forgiveness. In the second, draw what it feels like to be forgiven. If you can't forgive, imagine *what it would be like.*

Before forgiveness:

After forgiveness:

Alright, here are some questions to answer in writing:

Why is forgiving yourself important?

How can you hold onto self-forgiveness while maintaining responsibility for your actions? If you're not sure, search "healthy self-forgiveness" online and explore what you find.

DAY 26. PEOPLE IN YOUR LIFE

People People People People People People People People People PEOPLE People PEOPLE

PURPOSE OF THIS WORKSHEET:

- To identify the main players in your life
- To better understand each player's role

EVERYONE NEEDS PEOPLE, especially when healing from chemical dependency. Recovery can't happen in isolation. This worksheet helps you understand the role of friends and family in your life.

Using the example below as a guide, use the next page to map out the people in your life. Follow these instructions:

1. First, fill the page with names of family and friends. List the main players.
2. For each person, describe their role in your sobriety.

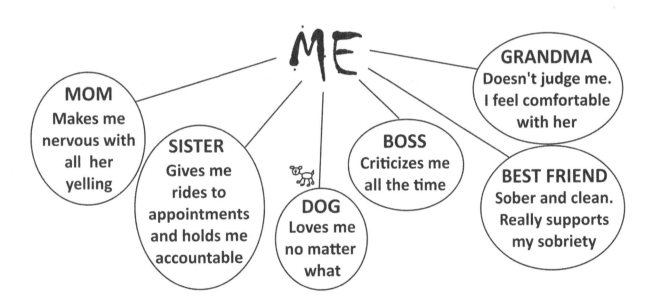

Now it's your turn. Go to the next page.

The Outside-the-Box Recovery Workbook

People People People People People People People People People PEOPLE People PEOPLE

Use the space below to map out the important people in your life.

3. Next, grab two highlighters, each a different color. Highlight all healthy relationships with one color. Highlight all unhealthy relationships with the other. If both, don't highlight.

REFLECTION

Look over your diagram. Are your relationships mostly healthy or unhealthy? Why?

How can you distance yourself from the unhealthy individuals in your life?

How can you better surround yourself with supportive people?

DAY 27. MAKING FRIENDS

PURPOSE OF THIS WORKSHEET:

- To explore the meaning of friendship
- To find ways to make friends

IMAGINE YOU'RE AN INMATE AT A FEDERAL PRISON. You've spent the past 20 years in jail for a crime you didn't commit.

This morning the warden appeared at your cell and announced you're free to go. The sentence was a mistake. To make up for it, you're being discharged to your own luxury house, with a fancy sports car and lifetime supply of cash.

Life seemed great… until now. You're sitting in a strange kitchen in a strange luxury house with nothing to do. You don't know anyone. You have no friends.

1. How can you meet new people?

2. Which of the following are BAD ways to find friends?

   a. Attend 12-step or SMART meetings.
   b. Engage in school or work.
   c. Stay in the house and read.
   d. Participate in worship or spiritual groups.
   e. Volunteer.
   f. Participate in community groups and clubs.
   g. Start using drugs.
   h. Go out but refuse to talk to anyone.
   i. Sign up for non-credit or community classes.
   j. Rob banks.
   k. Spend time at healthy hangouts (like cafes).
   l. Join a cause or movement.
   m. Travel and learn about new places.
   n. Meet people online.

FRIENDS

3. Over the next month you make two dozen friends. How do you do it?

   a. You step outside of your house, head for a café, sign-up for music lessons and a local hiking group, then work your way over to an art store. That night you attend Atheists Anonymous. This activity-hopping becomes an everyday thing. You're friendly and gracious and kind. You secretly help the homeless.
   b. You step out of your house, head for the local café, and don't talk to anyone. Ever.
   c. You stick to solitary activities: writing, jogging, etc. You don't talk to anyone.
   d. You have faith. Eventually friends will come along, even if you stay in your house all the time. Someone might knock at the front door.
   e. A is right, except you don't have to be so busy. You can do 5% of that and meet people.
   f. You don't leave the house but instead invite in anyone who'd like to visit, especially shady people you meet online.

4. How do you define friendship?

   a. A friend is always there for you and knows all your secrets.
   b. A friend is someone whose company you enjoy. You don't need to share all your secrets, but you see them often and care about them.
   c. Friends include "one-activity" people. You have one interest in common, something you both like, and that's all you talk about or do together. You see this friend often and enjoy their company.
   d. Friends include people you see because your schedules coincide, even though you don't formerly "get together." For example, a close colleague, hairdresser, or soccer coach.
   e. Everyone is a potential friend.
   f. Everyone is a friend.
   g. Friends? You don't want to know anything about friends.

ANSWERS

1. Answers will vary. See #2 for ideas.
2. C, G, H, J are all bad ideas. N can be a good or bad idea, depending on perspective and safety.
3. Answers are A and E. A is for the over-achiever, and E is perfectly acceptable. The trick is to get out of the house and involve yourself with others—in a safe way. F is considered dangerous.
4. Answers will vary. All except G can be defined as friendship, depending on your point of view. F is a matter of debate; some people say strangers are potential friends, but that's another conversation.

WE KNOW YOU DON'T NEED THEM, but here are some "friend-making" tips anyway.

- *Engage others and focus on THEM.* The best way to make friends is to show interest. Everybody wants to feel important. Make sure to listen. Ask questions. Be empathetic. Express understanding.
- *"Instant friendship" doesn't happen often.* Making friends can be a gradual, trial-and-error process, and you have to roll with the punches. It can take months to years to turn an acquaintance into a friend.
- *Be flexible.* Most mistakes are forgivable. You mess up a conversation? That's okay. There's probably room for repair. The other person inadvertently offends you? Be forgiving, if that's the right thing to do.
- *Have compassion.* Be kind. Don't criticize, belittle, or gossip. Look for people's strengths.
- *Finally, be yourself.* Above all, be yourself.

Please go to the next page. → → →

TO REMIND YOU TO BE YOURSELF, we've prepared the following word search puzzle. How many times can you find the words "BE YOURSELF?"

(Please see Appendix C for answers)

REFLECTION

This worksheet is about making friends. How do you hold onto friends once you have them?

What kind of qualities do you look for in a friend?

Some people have a large, multi-layered social circle. Others prefer one or two close friends. Which is your tendency? Why?

DAY 28. THE "YOU" IN RECOVERY

PURPOSE OF THIS WORKSHEET:

- To explore the question, "Who am I now that I'm in recovery?"

TO KNOW YOURSELF, you must know your *past* and how it leads to the present. Complete each box and follow the arrows. If needed, use a separate sheet of paper.

START HERE. Finish the sentence, "I miss drugs or alcohol at times because…"

How will you deal with the loss?

What are the benefits to recovery? (You've seen this one before too…)

Why are you quitting anyway? What don't you like about addiction? (You've answered this question a 1000 times before!)

List two strengths that were present before you went into recovery. They can be talents, skills, or abilities.

Name two weaknesses you want to change. (Don't be embarrassed to look at your weaknesses. The knowledge helps you grow.)

How can you use these strengths to help you stay clean?

How does understanding your past strengthen your recovery?

How does understanding these weaknesses help you stay clean?

Next page

➡ **CONTINUE HERE.**

We've focused on the past and how it led to the present.

Now we visit the *present*, with sails pointed toward the future.

Who is the "new" YOU in recovery? Follow the arrows and answer the questions to find out.

REFLECTION. *Things were different before recovery. You've changed. You've grown. Below, please introduce the new YOU to the world!*

My name is _____, and this is the new me! I am...

⬇

Pick 4 *positive* words that describe the new YOU since recovery.

1.   2.

3.   4.

⬆

Complete the following sentences without giving them too much thought:

1-A good memory since recovery is:

2-People I can call when I need company are:

3-One thing I look forward to in life is:

⬇

Apart from drugs, what makes you happy? What do you enjoy doing?

Who are your heroes? Why?

What can you do to work towards having these qualities yourself?

⬆

How does this new YOU want to impact the lives of others? (It's okay to start small.)

⬇

What does the new YOU need?

➡   ➡

DAY 29. THE BUCKET LIST

PURPOSE OF THIS WORKSHEET:

- To focus on dreams and goals for the future
- To make plans

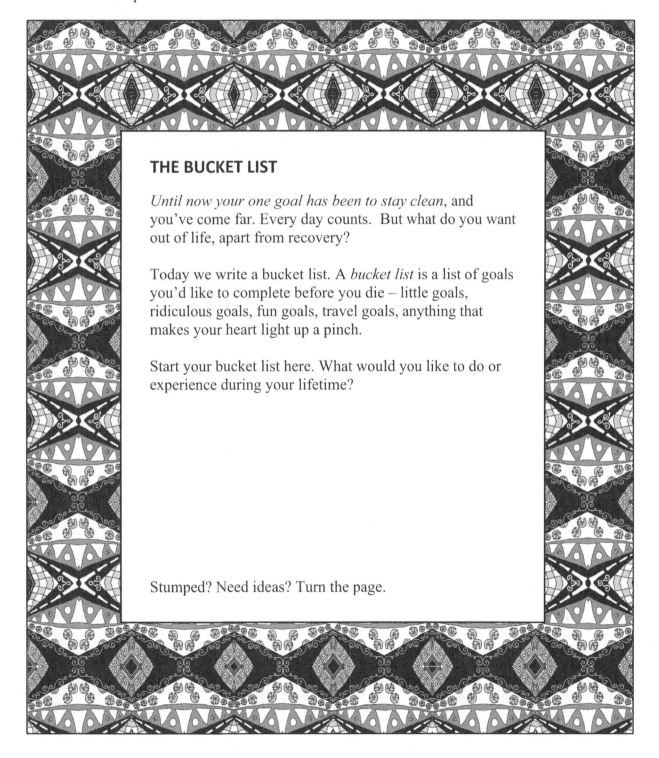

THE BUCKET LIST

Until now your one goal has been to stay clean, and you've come far. Every day counts. But what do you want out of life, apart from recovery?

Today we write a bucket list. A *bucket list* is a list of goals you'd like to complete before you die – little goals, ridiculous goals, fun goals, travel goals, anything that makes your heart light up a pinch.

Start your bucket list here. What would you like to do or experience during your lifetime?

Stumped? Need ideas? Turn the page.

MAKING A BUCKET LIST? See our ideas below.

	THE BUCKET LIST Check all activities that might interest you.	
☐ Make someone happy	☐ Reconnect with family	☐ Decorate your house
☐ Chase a storm	☐ Pet or own an iguana	☐ Build a card tower
☐ Learn to ride a bicycle	☐ Learn to ride a motorcycle	☐ Race motorcycles
☐ Take care of a betta fish	☐ Take care of an aquarium	☐ Build a pond
☐ Go fishing	☐ Buy a fishing boat	☐ Go ocean fishing
☐ Adopt a penguin	☐ No, don't adopt a penguin	☐ Adopt a cat or dog
☐ Train your dog	☐ Adopt a parrot	☐ Teach a parrot to talk
☐ Teach a parrot silence	☐ Teach a parrot to play dead	☐ Read and write better
☐ Read and write a novel	☐ Read something important	☐ Read Shakespeare
☐ Study history	☐ Study math	☐ Get your GED
☐ Finish high school	☐ Take a non-credit class	☐ Get a degree
☐ Become a teacher	☐ Become a professor	☐ Train dolphins
☐ Meditate every day	☐ Learn to levitate	☐ Become an expert
☐ Learn the lyrics to a song	☐ Memorize a poem	☐ Research religion
☐ Study Zen	☐ Learn martial arts	☐ Volunteer at a shelter
☐ Look for a job	☐ Find a job and work	☐ Find your dream job
☐ Open a business	☐ Invest in the stock market	☐ Learn to play guitar
☐ Collect watches or guitars	☐ Become a counselor	☐ Get your driver's license
☐ Own a car	☐ Own an expensive car	☐ Donate lots of money
☐ Make plans to be famous	☐ Become famous	☐ Be famous & wealthy
☐ Design a website	☐ Write a poem	☐ Learn a new language
☐ Learn a 3rd language	☐ Learn English properly	☐ Learn computer code

THE BUCKET LIST (CONTINUED)
Check all activities that might interest you.

☐ Become a photographer	☐ Attend church	☐ Become a minister
☐ Travel overseas	☐ Cook a big meal	☐ Try indoor skydiving
☐ Join the Peace Corp	☐ Learn to identify bird calls	☐ Learn to stop time
☐ Buy a house	☐ Build a house	☐ Buy an island
☐ Clean hiking trails	☐ Travel to your birthplace	☐ Find the perfect pie
☐ Go caving	☐ Hypnotize a chicken	☐ Fix a computer
☐ Take up gardening	☐ Go to a comics conference	☐ Make a fake volcano
☐ Make contact with aliens	☐ Make dollar bill gift trees	☐ Make boxes using paper
☐ Make boxes out of wood	☐ Make a piece of furniture	☐ Build a birdhouse
☐ Design a skyscraper	☐ Learn about Saturn	☐ Become an astronaut
☐ Buy junk from stores	☐ Visit Tibet	☐ Go dancing
☐ Write an autobiography	☐ Become an airplane pilot	☐ Get into shape
☐ Learn to juggle	☐ Make a chess set	☐ Learn to play chess
☐ Learn to read tarot	☐ Draw or paint	☐ Learn to play drums
☐ Learn to roller skate	☐ Start a farm	☐ Own a peacock
☐ Learn how to beatbox	☐ Learn to play cards	☐ Learn to play pool
☐ Take a cruise	☐ Learn to swim	☐ Ride a horse
☐ See a bullfight	☐ Go to a play	☐ Make your own clothes
☐ Go to Machu Picchu	☐ Go to India	☐ Go to China
☐ Go to Africa	☐ Dye hair purple	☐ Make this list longer

READY FOR THE NEXT STEP? Put aside all adult worries and be a kid for a moment. Choose one item on your list and create a comic strip about achieving that goal, drawing one step at a time. Use stick figures and comments in each frame. Let yourself be goofy.

REFLECTION

Plan to do at least one goal a week for the next month. Which goals do you choose? List them below and make them happen!

Week 1's goal	Week 2's goal
Week 3's goal	Week 4's goal

DAY 30. YOUR FUTURE IN RECOVERY

PURPOSE OF THIS WORKSHEET

- To celebrate recovery
- To explore what recovery means to you

WHAT DOES YOUR FUTURE IN RECOVERY LOOK LIKE? Sobriety, friends, travel, motorcycles, five children, a degree in anthropology? This worksheet helps to further clarify your future in recovery.

For this exercise you need:
- A poster board
- Old photos, magazines, books, online images, doodles, and other things that symbolize your goals in recovery
- Scissors and glue
- Optional: a copier and/or printer

INSTRUCTIONS: Gather pictures that symbolize recovery. Go through albums, magazines, and books. Search online. Doodle up a storm. Each time there's an inkling, each time a picture feels right, rip it out or make a copy and add it to the pile. If you have pictures from Day 14, include them here. Once you have enough, glue them to a poster board until the entire board is covered.

Next, stand back and *pay attention*. Study every line and color and detail. Consider each picture carefully, then choose one from the bunch. Sketch a copy of this picture in the box below. A basic outline is enough. Then answer the questions on the next page.

1. Why did you choose *this* picture?

2. What does the image mean to you? Is there a memory, dream, or something else behind it?

REFLECTION

You've caught a bit of recovery – and yourself – here in this book. Thank you! Put the recovery collage in an obvious spot and refer to it often. Study it until you've memorized every detail. That, friend, is your future.

According to your collage, what is your future in recovery about?

What can you do to work towards that future, starting today?

What to Do When You Finish the Book
And Resources

WHAT TO DO WHEN YOU FINISH THIS BOOK.

WHAT YOU FOUND (HOPEFULLY)

If our mad plan worked, you've completed this manual in one piece and had a whirlwind journey to boot. Which of the following is NOT part of the *Outside-the-Box Recovery Workbook*?

a. Learning about recovery
b. Understanding and pursuing change
c. Reading a story about an alien and an elephant
d. Learning about alter egos
e. Working in a coffee shop with difficult customers
f. Writing multiple-choice poetry
g. Exploring past, present, and future
h. Writing the beginnings of a movie
i. Understanding the importance of friends and family
j. Imagining you're a TV show host
k. A silly story about a mayor
l. Exploring change
m. Reading a tale about rose-colored glasses
n. Helping an addicted mayor
o. Writing a comic
p. Doing lots of hard work

What do you think? Options not found in this book include C, F, and M, each a subject found in the *OTB Recovery Workbook Part 2*.

All other subjects (A, B, D, E, G, H, I, J, K, L, N, O, and P) are in this book.

There's a lot we didn't go over:

- Delayed gratification
- Dealing with unnecessary drama
- Overcoming loss
- Rebelling in healthy ways
- Mindfulness
- Life skills
- Creativity
- Journaling
- Improving memory and thinking
- Problem-solving
- And much more…

Alas, there wasn't enough room!

These subjects and more are reserved for the upcoming *Outside-the-Box Recovery Workbooks 2 and 3*. Coming soon!

WHAT YOU'RE CLOSER TO (HOPEFULLY)

Here are some questions to consider:

Since quitting, what's filled the void in your life? (If you can't think of anything, see the Wish List on page 50 and the Bucket List, pages 89-92.)

What are you doing (or can you do) to make it happen?

WRAP-UP.

You've reached the end of your 30-day journey! It's been a crazy experience. Between comics, relapse prevention, alter egos, taking inventory, and writing movies, you've invested a lot of energy and absorbed plenty of information. You've processed mistakes. You've moved forward in recovery and established a foundation for your future. Please keep trying, keep fighting. It's hard work reaching the place you want to go, but it's oh-so-worthwhile. Whatever you do, make it a stunning ride.

Don't forget to keep an eye out for future *Outside-the-Box Recovery Workbooks*, more 30-day journeys of a lifetime. (Need more now? Check out page 126.)

RESOURCES FOR YOUR JOURNEY

BOOKS

Beaufort F (2017). *Recovery through creativity: Overcoming superhero syndrome.* Bloomington, IN: Balboa Press.

Glasner-Edwards S (2015). *The addiction recovery skills workbook: Changing addictive behaviors using CBT, mindfulness, and motivational interviewing techniques.* Oakland, CA: New Harbinger Publisher.

Kelly J, Benton B (2013). *Sober play: Using creativity for a more joyful recovery.* Portland, OR: 3 Cats Publishing.

Leonard L (1989). *Witness to the fire: Creativity and the veil of addiction.* Boston, MA: Shambhala Publications Inc.

Maisel E, Raeburn S (2008). *Creative recovery: A complete addiction treatment program that uses your natural creativity.* Boulder, CO: Trumpeter Books, an imprint of Shambhala Publications.

Mooney A (1992). *The recovery book.* New York, NY: Workman Publishing Company.

Smart Recovery (2013). *Smart recovery handbook 3rd edition: Tools and strategies to help you on your recovery journey.* Mentor, OH: Alcohol & Drug Abuse Self-Help Network, Inc dba SMART Recovery.

Spiegelman E, Stone M (2017). *The rewired workbook: A manual for addiction recovery.* Hobart, NY: Hatherleigh.

Williams R, Kraft J (2012). *The mindfulness workbook for addiction: A guide to coping with the grief, stress, and anger that trigger addictive behaviors.* Oakland, CA: New Harbinger.

ONLINE

12-Step Fun, "Step Work" (interesting resource with lovely illustrations):
http://www.the-twelve-steps.com/index.html

In the Rooms (resource for finding 12-step fellowship meetings and support):
https://www.intherooms.com/

Psychology Today (resource for finding a therapist):
http://www.psychologytoday.com

Substance Abuse Mental Health Association (resources including substance abuse crisis lines/online search for providers):
https://www.samhsa.gov/find-help/national-helpline

Appendices A-C

APPENDIX 1. DEALING WITH RELAPSE

RELAPSE? DO THE FOLLOWING:

1. Stop using.
2. Breathe and relax.
3. We said relax!
4. Color the next page.
5. Complete the following 5 pages.
6. Share with someone you trust.

DEALING WITH RELAPSE (P1)

Relapse? First, walk us through what happened. Answer the question in each box, then follow the arrows.

BEFORE. How were things going before this all started? What wasn't going well?

NEXT. What started the downward spiral? What happened next?

LAST STRAW. What finally made you relapse?

DEALING WITH RELAPSE (P3)
Here's an example.

What happened?

BEFORE: I live with my dad, who is always nasty and demeaning.

NEXT: I played basketball and took it too far. The next day my back hurt and I could hardly move. I thought the pain would never go away. I called the doctor's office. They had me on hold for ten minutes, and when I finally talked to the med assistant, she was hateful and said I was wasting her time.

LAST STRAW: Dad got home. He got on my case, said I was acting like an addict. So I thought, "What the hell? I should just go ahead and prove him right." That's when I went down to the basement and relapsed.

What can I do differently?

BEFORE: I need to surround myself with positive people and go to 12-step meetings.

NEXT: I should do things in moderation to avoid making the pain worse. I can change my thinking – "Really? The pain will never go away? Not true!" – The pain comes and goes. Better to think, "It sucks right now, but this isn't permanent."

I could have dealt differently with the med assistant. Rather than calling her bad names, I could have explained the situation calmly and asked (instead of demanded) to leave a message for the doctor.

LAST STRAW: I can learn to calm myself down no matter what the other person says. This is *my* recovery.

DEALING WITH RELAPSE (P4)

HERE ARE SOME CHANGES THAT PROMOTE RECOVERY
Check all that might be helpful

Immediate needs	
☐ If the relapse was severe, consider hospitalization. Get treatment if you have withdrawal symptoms.	☐ If the relapse was minor, pick yourself up and jump back into recovery.
☐ If you're struggling, consider a residential rehab.	☐ If you're okay but need extra support, consider a sober living setting.
☐ See an addiction counselor or therapist. Talk to your doctor about medications for addiction, depression, anxiety, etc.	☐ If you can't afford providers, contact a nonprofit clinic or the county mental health and substance abuse services.
☐ Attend a partial hospital or intensive outpatient program.	☐ Attend ninety 12-step meetings in ninety days. Contact your sponsor.
☐ Try not to be alone. Reach out to people who care about you.	☐ Call the SAMHSA crisis line 1-800-662-HELP for assistance and referrals.

Triggers or stressors	
☐ In general, avoid triggers. If you can't avoid a trigger, get away.	☐ Learn how to deal with stress without using. That means coping skills!
☐ If you live in a toxic situation, get out when you safely can. Consider a domestic violence shelter.	☐ If somebody is offensive, ignore, avoid or minimize contact with them. Don't waste your time with people who are toxic.
☐ To mend broken relationships, work on social skills, frustration tolerance, and assertiveness. Consider family therapy.	☐ If struggling with insecurity, spend time with people who make you feel good about yourself.
☐ If health or pain are an issue, work closely with your provider to get stable.	☐ If triggered by boredom or free time, get busy. Volunteer, study a language, clean the house, walk the dog, go cycling…
☐ For work problems, get support, switch to part-time, take a leave of absence, or join an Employee Assistance Program.	☐ If unemployed, attend vocational rehabilitation to receive assistance with application, interview, and job.
☐ For school problems, get tutoring, talk to the school counselor, change your schedule, or take a leave of absence.	☐ If lack of education is a trigger, work on your GED or get a professional certificate at your local community college.
☐ If you can't read, write, or do math, enroll in a free adult education class at your local community college.	☐ If access to easy money is a trigger, have someone else handle your finances. Get a representative payee.

DEALING WITH RELAPSE (P5)

Recovery Plan

Game plan. Using the information from pages 1-4, make a list of changes you're prepared to make to promote your recovery. Next to each change, describe what you need to do to make it happen. What can you do *today*?

Now go forth and make those changes!

APPENDIX B: A NOTE TO PROFESSIONALS

BACKGROUND

My name is Kim Rosenthal, MD. I'm a psychiatrist with over 2 decades of experience working in the mental health and substance use disorder fields. Professionally, I've worked in a variety of settings, including alcohol and substance abuse treatment centers (ADATC's), detox units, rehabs, day hospitals, clinics, inpatient hospitalization, forensic hospitals, and veteran healthcare.

As a physician, I practice evidence-based medicine and conform strictly to the standard of care. As a multi-modal professional, I believe in the power of therapeutic interaction and the many disciplines needed to help people with addiction. Relapse prevention is important. 12-step programming, cognitive behavioral therapy, motivational interviewing, Matrix Model, psychoeducation, and coping skill training are all important. These are just some of the modalities we use to take on substance use disorders, and studies show they make a difference.

But there's room for more. We need more. In the age of COVID, where isolation and addiction are more rampant than ever, we desperately need evidence-based treatment options that are… well, outside-the-box. That means narrative therapy. It also means artwork, creative writing, positive psychology, and humor. Why outside-the-box? Because it works! Research shows that combining mainstream treatment with these extra approaches increase retention and lower relapse rate (Beaufort 2017; Eschleman et al 2014; McKay 2016). That means we can improve patient outcome by supplementing mainstream care with optimism, creativity, art, and a pinch of humor.

COMBINING TRADITIONAL AND EVIDENCE-BASED NON-TRADITIONAL TREATMENT IMPROVES RETENTION AND LOWERS RELAPSE RATE.

Examples of Traditional Approaches	*Examples of Nontraditional Approaches*
Motivational interviewing	Art therapy
Relapse prevention	Narrative therapy
Cognitive behavioral therapy	Expressive therapy
Matrix model	Creative writing
Mindfulness	Poetry therapy
Psychoeducation	Positive psychology
Coping and life skills training	Cognitive remediation
Medication management	Coloring mindfulness
Strength-based treatment	Journaling
Contingency management	Humor

The *Outside-the-Box Recovery Workbook* combines both traditional and non-traditional in one book. It's written for addiction counselors and their clients – and anyone in early recovery. Worksheets take on common themes, including:

- Reasons for quitting
- Consequences of using
- Understanding addiction and recovery
- Identifying triggers/taking on cravings
- Making change
- Dealing with war stories
- Processing past mistakes
- Understanding healthy relationships
- Making friends

That's traditional stuff, yes, but recovery is more than staying sober. It's more than combining mainstream with outside-the-box. Recovery is about creating a new identity, and "new" isn't pathological. "New" needs silliness and exploration. It needs joy. It means learning to love life without drugs and alcohol. Coloring, movie-writing, alter egos, letters, puzzles, collages, cartoons, odd multiple-choice questions, and jokes? It all matters.

GENERAL INFORMATION

The *Outside-the-Box Recovery Workbook* is the first in a three-part series. (We're still working on the second two parts.) There are 30 worksheets, each 2-4 pages in length. At the beginning of the book you'll find a Relapse Prevention Plan. The end includes a section about relapse. Here are some general recommendations.

- For individual work, the manual can be followed from beginning to end; it's self-explanatory and doesn't have to involve a professional. However, recovery doesn't happen in isolation. We need people, and anyone dealing with a substance use disorder can benefit from professional guidance.
- For drug & alcohol counselors and their clients, the workbook may be used as primary therapist-driven treatment or to augment other approaches. Unless otherwise indicated, most worksheets can stand alone and be used in any order.
- Almost all handouts can be completed during a single session.
- Clients should be encouraged to do the exercises in writing.
- Review the Reflection Section at the end of each worksheet to promote thought and anchor important points. For groups, these final questions can prompt important conversation.
- We recommend reviewing the relapse prevention plan often – every session, if necessary. It's important that clients overlearn the material rather than rely on reading it during weak moments.
- There are five "Take-a-Break" and two mindful coloring worksheets in the book. These can be used at the beginning or end of a session to "get people going" or as optional homework. (We'd be honored if coloring sheets are colored in and hung somewhere in your practice!)

RECOMMENDATIONS FOR SPECIFIC HANDOUTS

- **Day 1. Why Did You Quit?** *Relapse prevention (Hendershot et al 2011; Rawson et al 2005; Witkiewitz et al 2007), letter writing (Bolton, 2004).* This handout reminds clients why they chose recovery and aims to bolster resolve. Open the session by asking each person to write a list of reasons they quit. Next, review the ideas in the worksheet and have clients supplement their list. When ready, give the group 15-20 minutes to write the letters. Consider handing out stationery and playing music. Afterwards, use these letters to jumpstart discussion, asking, "How can you use this to promote recovery in the future?" "Why is it important to believe what you write?" "What can you do to improve your letter?" Some clients might want to share what they wrote. To extend this exercise, have the group supplement their letter with photos, drawings, and stickers, then put it in an envelope and mail it to themselves. The effect can be powerful and an excellent motivator. (We explore reasons for quitting further in the book, especially Days 4, 6, and 25).

- **Day 2. Opinions and Trivia.** *Psychoeducation (Bhattacharjee et al, 2011).* This worksheet promotes conversation about substance use disorders, side effects, consequences of using, and ways to overcome addiction. Pick at least one or two of the questions for discussion and review the T/F statements. To take this a step further, consider having each client create one true and one false statement about the negative effects of drugs (statistics, side effects, mortality rate) and challenge the group to determine which is true. They should use their smart phones to find and verify information. Finally, elicit several methods people use to *overcome* substance use disorders. Once you have a list, move onto the next page and discuss the puzzle search terms, each a method or motivator to get past chemical dependency. Encourage clients to complete the puzzle.

- **Day 3. The YOU Before It All Happened.** *Narrative therapy (Diamond, 2002; Gardner, 2009; Garte-Wolf, 2011).* Narrative therapy helps a person distance themselves from an issue, enough to examine it more objectively. Open up discussion by asking, "Imagine you met the Past You from before you started using. What would that be like?" After a brief chat, have client answer the first five questions in the handout. (Consider having clients write a dialogue describing the interaction between their past and present. They should include details about facial expressions and gestures – and bonus points for revealing thoughts, emotions, and inner dialogue!) Focus on the reflection for continued discussion and take-home points. How have they changed as a person, both good and bad? What have they learned from their experience?

- **Day 4. The Effects of Substance Abuse.** *Relapse prevention, cognitive therapy.* Day 4 continues to explore the question, "Why quit drugs?" It also helps clients identify level of contentedness in their lives and reframes the challenges of having "room for improvement." Consider drawing the first diagram or wheel on the board and answering questions as a group. Brain-storm negative consequences for each section in the pie chart. The second diagram is best done individually. Clients should rate their level of happiness for each category then chart it in the wheel. An example is provided on the next page. Review reflection questions together. The heartache of chemical dependency and positives of recovery are themes throughout the book.

- **Day 5. Describing Addiction Through Art.** *Art therapy (Aletraris, 2014; Matto 2002, 2003; Sharp, 2018; Wilson, 2012), creative therapy (Beautfort, 2017; Eschleman et al, 2014).* This worksheet uses art therapy to better understand addiction; processing problems in a nonverbal way can promote insight exponentially. Give the group 20-30 minutes to complete their drawing. Offer paper, crayons, colored pencils, markers, stickers, etc. If needed, find examples online by searching for "art about addiction." Make it clear that illustrations should *not* include drawings of drugs or drug paraphernalia. When finished, review the reflection questions. Inquire about emotions and thoughts as related to the drawing, as well as any new insights. Clients can share their work if desired. People often feel uncomfortable at first with this exercise but amaze themselves with the results.

- **Days 6 and 7. Relationship with Addiction Parts 1-2.** *Narrative therapy, creative writing (Dingle G et al, 2017; Pinhasi-Vittorio et al, 2018; Snead et al, 2015; Williamson C et al, 2018).* These two worksheets create space between addiction and self to improve the client's understanding of their relationship with chemical dependency. The handouts also provide an opportunity to mentally prepare for success. They can be done individually, or divide clients into groups, each group writing their own movie. After movies have been shared, go over the reflection questions and ask what they've learned. How did it feel to see their problem from a distance? Did they see things differently? What was it like to beat addiction?

- **Day 8. What is Recovery?** *Psychoeducation, narrative therapy.* This worksheet clarifies the difference between abstinence and recovery. Start out by asking, "What's the difference between quitting and being in recovery?" Have your client(s) answer questions 1-3 on their own. Once finished, review the answers and spend a good portion of the session discussing the reflection questions. Define "dry drunk" and help clients understand that addictive behaviors can happen even when clean and sober.

- **Day 9. Identifying Triggers.** *Relapse prevention.* This worksheet serves to (1) identify triggers and (2) emphasize trigger avoidance, especially in early recovery. Start the session by asking clients about their triggers and how they deal with them. Next, have the clients review the worksheet checklist and add any additional triggers to their list. Discuss the importance of avoiding triggers. Have clients give examples of when they've said NO or could have benefitted from saying NO. Finally ask the group, "But what do you do when you can't avoid a trigger?" (The answer to this final question is explored on Day 10.) The rest of the session can be used completing the word search.

- **Day 10. Dealing with Unavoidable Triggers.** *Narrative therapy, relapse prevention.* Day 10 explores triggers and trigger management. Come up with a list of triggers (or borrow them from Day 9) and write them on the board. Next, review the worksheet together. Identify ways to deal with all five of the mayor's triggers. Finally, review the list of triggers on the board and brainstorm ways to manage each one. To take it a step further, ask "What do you think about a politician having an addiction? What if it were your doctor, lawyer, priest?" "Would they see a doctor who was actively using? How about one who hasn't used for a week?" Explore their responses and the fact that drugs affect all walks of life.

- **Days 11 and 12. Getting Past Cravings 1-2.** *Relapse prevention.* These two worksheets take on cravings. For the first session, start by asking, "What are cravings?" and "How do *you* deal with them?" Review questions 1-3 and the "got cravings" flowchart, then discuss the two urge-management techniques listed. Clients are encouraged to monitor cravings and practice the techniques before meeting next time, documenting their experience. Review what they practiced at the next session. If they didn't do the homework, spend a good few minutes going over the advantages and disadvantages of doing homework. How motivated are they to skip the important stuff? Enjoy the process but pay special attention to those who did complete the task. Next, review the terms listed for the crossword puzzle. The answers to the puzzle are a list of urge-management techniques. Finally, before the next session, have clients practice two urge-management techniques and report back later. This time, if they don't do the homework, consider having them "practice" in class. For example, "You're in line at the supermarket. The clerk is an old using buddy. You have a craving. How do you deal with it?" or "Your aunt is pestering you. You're angry and feel that drugs can calm you down. You have a craving…" Consider having clients stand up and act out each scenario.

- **Days 13-15. Grieving the Loss of Addiction 1-3.** *Motivational interviewing (Miller 2012), goal-management training (Alfonso, 2011), letter writing, narrative therapy, positive psychology (Hoeppner B 2018; Krentzman, 2013).* This set of worksheets will take 2-3 sessions to complete. The first (Day 13) uses motivational interviewing to weigh the pro's and con's of using – to better understand recovery. Open discussion by asking, 'What do you like about using?" "What are the problems?" Give clients time to answer the questions in writing and come up with a letter before posing several important questions: "What is it like breaking up with addiction?" "Is breaking up once enough?" Day 14 can be used for homework. Alternatively, devote a class to the journaling option. The final worksheet in the series, Day 15, uses goal-management training and positive psychology to help the client replace drugs with something worthwhile. Make sure to review Day 14 exercises. Next, promote conversation by asking, "If a genie grants you a long-term wish, what would you wish for? Really? Why?" After discussion, have clients complete the worksheet. Discuss the importance of replacing drugs with passions. We all need something to look forward to. Pursuing goals will be explored more on Days 29 and 30.

- **Day 16. Introducing Change.** *Relapse prevention, change (DiClemente 2018), matrix model, narrative therapy.* This worksheet introduces change. First ask, "Why is change important for recovery?" After discussion and reviewing the body of the worksheet, offer a few examples of changed stories like the example provided, and give clients 20 minutes to change their own story or song. Alternatively, consider presenting a specific song (like lyrics from the Stones or Beatles) and have everyone rewrite it and share. Change is explored further on Days 17-20.

- **Day 17. Change What You Do.** *Relapse prevention, change, matrix model, narrative therapy.* With their dominant hand, have clients write the phrase, "This is how I usually do things," then write, "I never do things this way, this is crazy" with their non-dominant hand. Discuss the difficulty associated with change. Ask "So what kinds of life changes do you need to make for recovery to work?" "What can't be changed?" Use the worksheet to promote discussion, finally emphasizing ways to deal with problems beyond one's control. Possibilities include adaptation, unconditional acceptance, and mindfulness.

- **Day 18. Change How You Talk.** *Relapse prevention, behavioral therapy/change, matrix model, narrative therapy.* This worksheet takes on war talk. Ask clients what they know about addiction war stories. Next, review the questions and end with the reflection section.

- **Days 19-20. Change and Alter Ego Parts I-II.** *Cognitive behavioral therapy/change, narrative therapy.* These worksheets further explore change and goals. For Day 19, ask clients, "What does completed recovery look like?" "How do you know when you're in recovery?" "What's the end goal?" Explain that in this handout an alter ego (AE) is an ideal version of their futures in recovery: same past, perfect outcome. Each client should use the worksheet to create their own AE. Day 20 helps clients stand back and see what realized recovery looks like. Have them consider the scenarios individually then compare their answers as a group. The reflection sparks discussion about the ideal self and how this concept can be used to clarify goals. An AE can be a useful tool to promote growth and deal with problems.

- **Day 21. Addiction's Effect on Others.** *Social support (Stevens, 2015).* Day 21 introduces past mistakes, in this case addiction's effect on those we care about. The focus is empathy – and an introduction to Days 22 and 23, where mistakes are further identified and processed. Encourage each client to describe the influence drugs had/have on those around them. Next, grab a timer. Tell them, "Now you're going to draw a picture of someone in your life who was affected by your addiction. You have five minutes. Focus on that one person the whole time. Try to understand what it was like for them." Repeat the process in 5-minute increments, each time a new person, as time allows. Remind them to include themselves.

- **Day 22. The Interview: Recognizing Mistakes.** *Narrative therapy, 12-step* (Alcoholics Anonymous World Services 1989). Day 22 examines past mistakes. Clients are asked to describe in detail three things they regret doing. Start by reading the worksheet together, then use the rest of the session to have the group answer the questions in writing. This is a difficult exercise and might take more than one session – or can be finished as homework. The next handout provides the opportunity to process mistakes.

- **Day 23. After the Interview: Mistakes and Hope.** *Narrative therapy, 12-step.* This worksheet helps clients begin to right past wrongs. Review the prior handout (Day 22), or have clients identify 3 errors from their past, then ask, "How do you deal with these mistakes?" Discuss possible ways to "right wrongs," reminding clients that making up for the past takes time. Next, review worksheet 23. The task is to write a fake "Letter to the Editor" outlining what can be done to right past wrongs. Consider sharing samples first, something like, "Dear Editor, I regret stealing from my wife. I make up for this mistake by not relapsing. I'm respectful, honest, and take care to not repeat the act." When everyone has completed the letter, review the reflection questions together.

- **Day 24. Dealing with Unforgiveable Mistakes.** *Coping skills (Roos, 2016), cognitive behavioral therapy/change.* This handout is an important one: how to deal with past wrongs when forgiveness isn't available. Review the worksheet with your client(s), spending most of your time on questions 3-6. Everyone should answer the reflection individually before discussing different ways to right wrongs that leave them hanging.

- **Day 25. Self-Forgiveness.** *Coping skills, forgiveness (Webb, 2015).* Day 25 takes on self-forgiveness without shirking responsibility for past mistakes. Forgiveness doesn't mean forgetting. Ask, "What is it like to be forgiven? What is it like to forgive?" Clients write a letter forgiving themselves for past transgressions while holding onto the lessons these actions have taught them. Review the reflection questions together.

- **Day 26. People in Your Life.** *Social support.* Day 26 is the first of two worksheets about the importance of social support and friendship. Ask, "Why do we need people? What kinds of people promote recovery? What kinds make it harder?" Clients map out the important people in their lives, including each person's influence on their recovery. Discuss ways to increase healthy relationships and avoid/handle unhealthy ones. If clients are uncertain, encourage them to research online and report back with their findings.

- **Day 27. Making Friends.** *Social support.* This handout explores ways to make friends. Ask, "Recovery can be lonely. How do you make friends?" Your clients can review the worksheet individually then discuss answers as a group or read together and review one point at a time.

- **Day 28. The New You in Recovery.** *Motivational interviewing, relapse prevention, positive psychology.* This worksheet explores past and present to promote an understanding of their place in recovery. It also identifies recovery as a source of a new and improved identity. Ask, "Recovery means you're establishing a sober identity, but what does that mean? Who are you now that you're not using?" After listening to answers, clients answer the worksheet questions individually. When complete, encourage each person to share their final statement, "Hello, my name is _____, and this is the new me. I am_____"

- **Day 29. The Bucket List.** *Goal-management training.* Sobriety creates a hole in one's life, an empty space that needs to be filled. Day 29 starts this process with a bucket list. Ask, "What's on your bucket list? What would you like to do before you die?" Each individual should write their own list, supplementing their goals with ideas from the worksheet. Ask, "But how do you make these goals happen?" An important notion is breaking goals down into steps and starting with step one. Give examples. Clients should choose one goal and complete the comic or write out the steps before discussing the reflection as a group. (Note: goal-management training, problem-solving, and breaking tasks down into steps are explored further in the *Outside-the-Box Recovery Workbook Part 2*).

- **Day 30. Your Future in Recovery.** *Positive psychology.* Day 30 is a nonverbal way to explore the meaning of recovery. Bring magazines, posterboards, scissors, and glue for this exercise. Ask, "How do you know when you've officially recovered? What would your life be like?" These are hard question. Unlike Days Days 19-20, where clients explore their own identity, this exercise takes on life as a whole. Encourage clients to find pictures representing what that recovery would look like. After making and sharing their collages, client(s) choose one image and follow the instructions. Use the final 15 minutes to go over the reflection questions.

- **What to Do When You Finish This Book.** *Goal-management training, positive psychology.* The first part of this worksheet serves as a review. For the second part, ask clients, "What has replaced addiction in your life? What has fills that void?" Use the worksheet questions to guide the discussion and finish with the biggest question of all, "What can you do today to start the process?"

- **Appendix A, What to Do If You Relapse.** *Dialectical behavioral therapy chain analysis* (Linehan, 2015), *relapse prevention.* This worksheet is written for clients who slip up or relapse. Relapse is seen as a glitch in one's recovery plan. Between open-ended questions and check lists, the handout helps the reader examine recent events and make changes. It can be used repeatedly with the same client.

APPENDIX C: ANSWERS

DAY 1, PAGE 9. NUMBER OF DOGS IS ELEVEN.

DAY 2, PAGE 13. WORD SEARCH "OVERCOMING DRUGS"

```
        C A M P R A L     N O I T A C U D E
G             D A Y P R O G R A M             N
  E D E C I D E     R S                       O
I N T E N S I V E O U T P A T I E N T S
  N Y O H         B B             N           I
  T T   A E       A O     D       Y     O     R
  E E     C L     T X     E       T S   C     P
  R I       C P   I O     T T H E R A P Y
  V R R     O E   O N   O     F E S     M
  E B O     P     S E N E   X   A H H   E
  N O T     I     S S           S T O   T
  T S C     N       T U         G O N   H
  I E O     G         O T       N P E   A
  O S D     S           D N     I L S   D
  N O E     K             R O   K E T   O
    O E G N I F R U S E G R U D E H Y   N
    H S     L             G E           E
    C       L         T W E L V E S T E P S
            S         E S U B A T N A
H I T B O T T O M
```

TAKE A BREAK "PLEASE PICK A CARTOON," PAGE 25.

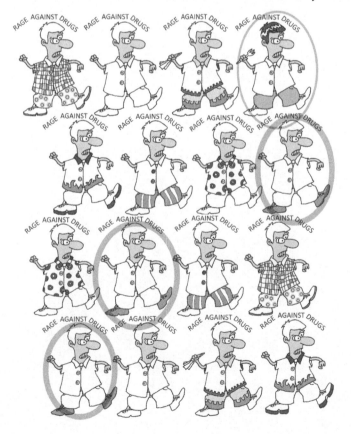

The Outside-the-Box Recovery Workbook

DAY 9, PAGE 33. WORD SEARCH "AVOID TRIGGER" (TERM APPEARS 9 TIMES).

A	A	R	E	G	G	I	R	T	D	I	O	V	A	
	V		R									V		R
R	O	O		E						O		E	E	
E	I		I		G				I		G		G	
G	D		D		G			D		G			G	
G	T			T		I	T		I				I	
I	R				R	R	R						R	
R	I			I	I	T	T						T	
T	G		G		D	G		D					D	
D	G		G	I			G		I				I	
I	E	E		O				E		O			O	
O	R	R	V						R		V		V	
V		A										A		
A	R	E	G	G	I	R	T	D	I	O	V	A		

DAY 12, PAGE 43. CROSSWORD PUZZLE "GETTING PAST CRAVINGS."

			A								
			L		C		T	A	L	K	
D			O		O		R				P
I			N		P		I				R
S		M	E	E	T	I	N	G			O
T		E		N		G		C			B
R	A	V	O	I	D		G		E		R	L
A		I					R	E	L	A	P	S	E
C									V		M
T		S	T	O	P						
		A				R	E	V	I	E	W
		T						N			
		E	X	E	R	C	I	S	E	G	

119

TAKE A BREAK PLEASE "RECOVERY MAZE," PAGE 44.

SOLVE THIS CODE PLEASE, PAGE 51.

"I've got 99 problems, and I'm all of them."

SOLVE THIS PUZZLE PLEASE WORD SEARCH "SOBER," PAGE 67. (TERM FOUND 16 TIMES).

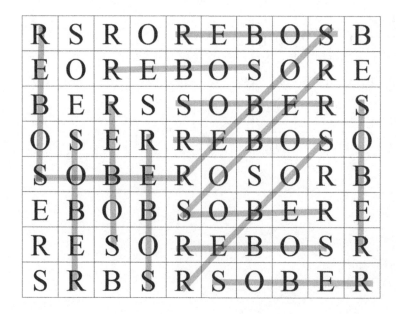

TAKE A BREAK PLEASE WORD SEARCH "TIPS FOR RECOVERY," PAGE 75.

A	S	T	A	Y	C	L	E	A	N	A	N	D	S	O	B	E	R	C
V	R				H							G		A				E
O	S	E	E	S	E	L	F	A	S	N	O	N	U	S	E	R	R		G
I			W			F	N					T		E				N
D				O			I	G			S		F					A
U		B			P			N		E	U		O			S		H
S		E				L			D	P	H	R				E		C
I	R	H		M			L			P	H	S	A	Y	N	O	L	O
N	E	O		A				I	O		E	O		B		U		T
G	B	N		K				R	W	L			B		I	R		N
F	O	O		E		T		F	N			B		T		D		E
R	S	R	E	G	G	I	R	T	D	I	O	V	A		I	S	N	P
I	N	A		O						Y			E		E	O	
E	U	B		A							L			S	B		E
N	F	L		L		E	N	J	O	Y	L	I	F	E		T		B
D	E	E	S	P	A	L	E	R	D	N	A	T	S	R	E	D	N	U
S	V		I	M	P	R	O	V	E	S	K	I	L	L	S	T		O
		A	D	E	A	L	W	I	T	H	C	R	A	V	I	N	G	D
		H	G	N	I	K	N	I	H	T	E	V	I	T	A	G	E	N	O	N
P	R	A	C	T	I	C	E	H	O	N	E	S	T	Y				D

DAY 27, PAGE 86. WORD SEARCH, "BE YOURSELF" (TERM FOUND 13 TIMES).

		B					F	L	E	S	R	U	O	Y	E	B
F	B		E		B		F	F							E		E
L	E	B	F	Y		E		L	L					Y			Y
E	Y	E	L		O		Y		E	E			O				O
S	O	Y	E			U		O		S	S		U				U
R	U	O	S				R		U		R	R					R
U	R	U	R					S		R	S	U	U				S
O	S	R	U						E	E	S		O	O			E
Y	E	S	O					L	L		E			Y	Y		L
E	L	E	Y				F			F		L		E	E		F
B	F	L	E	S	R	U	O	Y	E	B			F		B		B
		F	B				F	L	E	S	R	U	O	Y	E	B	F

Other Stuff

REFERENCES

- Alcoholics Anonymous World Services, Inc (1989). *Twelve Steps and Twelve Traditions*. New York, NY: Alcoholics Anonymous World Services.
- Aletraris L, Paino M, Edmond M, Roman P, Bride B (2014). The use of art and music therapy in substance abuse treatment programs. *Journal of Addictions Nursing* 25(4): 190-196.
- Alfonso J, Caracuel A, Delgado-Pastor L, Verdejo-Garcia A (2011). Combined goal management training and mindfulness meditation improve executive functions and decision-making performance in abstinent polysubstance abusers. *Drug and Alcohol Dependence* 117(1): 78-81.
- Bhattacharjee D, Rai A, Singh N, Kumar P, Munda S, Das B (2011). Psychoeducation: A measure to strengthen psychiatric treatment. *Delhi Psychiatry Journal* 14(1): 33-39
- Beaufort F (2017). *Recovery Through Creativity: Overcoming Superhero Syndrome*. Bloomington, IN: Balboa Press.
- Bolton G, Howlett S, Lago C, Wright J (2004). *Writing cures: An Introductory Handbook of Writing in Counseling and Therapy*. Abingdon, Oxon (England): Routledge Publishers.
- Diamond J (2002). *Narrative Means to Sober Ends: Treating Addiction and its Aftermath*. New York/London: Guilford Press.
- DiClemente C (2018). *Addiction and Change: How Addiction Develops and Addicted People Recover,* 2nd edn. New York, NY: Guilford Substance Abuse.
- Dingle G, Williams E, Jetten J, Welch J (2017). Choir singing and creative writing enhance emotion regulation in adults with chronic mental health conditions. *British Journal of Clinical Psychology* 56: 4.
- Eschleman K, Madsen J, Alarcon G, Barelka A (2014). Benefiting from creative activity: The positive relationships between creative activity, recovery experiences, and performance-related outcomes. *Journal of Occupational and Organizational Psychology* 87(3): 579-598.
- Gardner P, Poole J (2009). One story at a time: Narrative therapy, older adults, and addictions. *Journal of Applied Gerontology* 28(5): 600-620.
- Garte-Wolf S(2011). Narrative therapy group work for chemically dependent clients with HIV/AIDS. *Social Work with Groups* 34: 330-338.
- Hendershot C, Witkiewitz K, George W, Marlatt GA (2011). Relapse prevention for addictive behaviors. *Substance Abuse Treatment, Prevention, and Policy* 6:17.
- Hoeppner B, Schick M, Carlon H, Hoeppner S (2018). Do self-administered positive psychology exercises work in persons in recovery from problematic substance use? An online randomized survey. *Journal of Substance Abuse Treatment* 99: 16-23.
- Krentzman, A (2013). Review of the application of positive psychology to substance use, addiction, and recovery research. *Psychology of Addictive Behaviors* 27(1): 151-165.
- Linehan M (2015). *DBT Skills Training Manual, 2nd edition*. New York, NY: Guilford Press.
- Matto H (2002). Integrating art therapy methodology in brief inpatient substance abuse treatment in adults. *Journal of Social Work Practice in the Addictions* 2(2): 69-83.
- Matto H, Corcoran J, Fassler A (2003). Integrating solution-focused and art therapies for substance abuse treatment: Guidelines for practice. *The Arts in Psychotherapy* 30: 265-272.
- McKay, J (2016). Making the hard work of recovery more attractive for those with substance use disorders. *Addiction Debate* 112(5).

- Miller W, Rollnick S (2012). *Motivational interviewing: Helping people change,* 3rd edn. New York, NY: Guildford Press
- Pinhasi-Vittorio (2018). Writing, sharing, and healing: The interplay of literacy in the healing journey of the recovering from substance abuse. *Journal of Poetry Therapy* 31(4): 209-223.
- Rawson R, Obert J, McCann M, Ling W (2005). *The Matrix Model Intensive Outpatient Alcohol and Drug Treatment Program.* Center City, MN: Hazelden Information and Educational Services.
- Roos C, Witkiewitz K (2016). Adding tools to the toolbox: The role of coping repertoire in alcohol treatment. *Journal of Consulting and Clinical Psychology* 84(7): 599-611.
- Sharp M (2018). Art therapy and the recovery process: A literature review. *Expressive Therapies Capstone Theses* 30.
- Snead B, Pakstis D, Evans B, Nelson R (2015). The use of creative writing interventions in substance abuse treatment. *Therapeutic Recreation Journal* 49(2): 179-182.
- Stevens E, Jason L, Ram D, Light J (2015). Investigating social support and network relationships in substance use disorder recovery. *Substance Abuse* 36(4): 396-399.
- Webb J, Hirsch J, Toussaint L (2015). Forgiveness as a positive psychotherapy for addiction and suicide: Theory, research, and practice. *Spirituality in Clinical Practice* 2(1): 48-60.
- Williamson C, Wright J (2018). How creative does writing have to be to be therapeutic? A dialogue on the practice and research of writing to recovery and survive. *Journal of Poetry Therapy* 31(2): 113-123.
- Wilson M (2012). Art therapy in addictions treatment: Creativity and shame reduction. In C. Malchiodi (Ed.), *Handbook of Art Therapy* (pp. 302-319). New York, NY: Guilford Press.
- Witkiewitz K, Marlatt GA (2007). Overview of relapse prevention. In Witkiewitz K, Marlatt, GA, *Evidence-Based Relapse Prevention* (pp3-18). Burlington, VA: Academic Press.

ABOUT THE AUTHOR

Kim Rosenthal, MD, started out wanting to become an arm-flailing, humored "live-life!" college professor.

She had it all planned. She would ride a motorcycle to class each day, wearing steampunk goggles and a long flowing scarf. With a whirl of questions, she'd invite her students to laugh and think and share life exponentially. She wanted to see people reach for their potential, wanted to be part of that journey – and eventually Rosenthal chose something even better. She devoted herself to helping people get past mental illness and addiction.

Much of Rosenthal's career as a psychiatrist has involved living out of a suitcase. Her journey as a travelling doc has led her from countryside to big cities to places where no one speaks English. Over the past 20 years, she's participated in the lives of tens of thousands of patients. She's worked at detox units, rehabs, hospitals, forensic settings, day programs, clinics, nursing homes, and caring for veterans. Rosenthal is board-certified by the American Board of Psychiatry and Neurology and holds medical licenses in North Carolina, Hawaii, and Maine. She's also founder of the *Outside-the-Box Recovery* movement, which she hopes will someday save the world and end all suffering. (It's a process, anyway! For now, the first step is to help people with addiction.)

The author believes that a mental health provider's role is to support others through life's darker moments. Psychiatry is, after all, the art of alleviating suffering. But it is in knowing that each person is unique, that our minds can't simply be stuffed into the diagnostic boxes we find in our textbooks, that the real work begins: a good clinician takes off their jacket, sits down, listens to what the client has to say, and seeks to hear of their passions and strengths as much as their struggles. We seek *joy* amidst the shadows.

These days Rosenthal works in a hospital in North Carolina. In her free time, she lives in the country with her husband, where she wards off bears with a stick and dreams about motorcycles, Steampunk goggles, and flowing scarves.

FINAL WORDS

WAS THIS BOOK HELPFUL? Are you looking for more *Outside-the-Box Recovery* material? Check out the *SECOND OTB Recovery Workbook,* available on Amazon. It uses poetry, art, maps, journaling, and communication with the past for a fresh journey into early recovery.

Alright, there's more. Kimrosenthalmd.com features 120+ articles and a dozen recovery worksheets and booklets, including titles like:

- Biopsy of a Relapse
- Getting Past Cravings and Life
- Mindfulness: Physical Sensations
- Replacing Drugs with the Good Stuff
- When You're Too Depressed to Think
- Please Don't Give Beer to Moose and Other True/False Questions

This recovery material is easily downloadable, and much of it is **FREE**. Subscribe to the website and you'll also receive a complimentary, abridged copy of the *Step One* booklet, retail valued at $57,999! You'll also get updates on freebies and future books.

Dr. Kim is super-excited about the *Outside-the-Box Recovery* movement. She figures if one person's life can be saved, all the drawing and writing and bad jokes are worth it. So far, her humble booklets have traveled a long way. They've shown up in state and federal facilities, private hospitals, day programs, prisons, clinics, and rehabs all over the United States -- and as far away as Australia and South Africa! Thanks to everyone who's been part of this endeavor. Truth is, we're just starting, and together we've got millions and millions of lives to save!

Until next time,

KIM ROSENTHAL, MD
KIMROSENTHALMD.COM

WHO ARE YOU? WHERE ARE YOU?
THE "ABOUT-THE-READER" QUESTIONNAIRE

You've spent the past 130 pages exploring our world. We'd love to hear about yours! Please complete this form and send it our way. Include your name and email address if you want us to be part of your family or vice versa (i.e. be on our mailing list). Thanks!

Name _____

Email address _____

Where are you? _____

Tell us about yourself.   ☐ Provider   ☐ Client

Why did you read this book?

☐ I'm a professional   ☐ I needed help   ☐ I was forced
☐ I'm in recovery   ☐ Fascinating reading   ☐ What? This is a book?

Out of the following, which would you like to see in future workbooks?

☐ Drawing exercises   ☐ Quizzes   ☐ Positive psychology
☐ CBT/Matrix Model   ☐ More scenarios   ☐ Online links
☐ Mindfulness   ☐ Creative writing   ☐ Find the odd man out
☐ Healing relationships   ☐ Philosophical reflection   ☐ Stages or recovery
☐ Improving cognition   ☐ Coping skills   ☐ Cartoons
☐ Puzzles & coloring   ☐ Cat-training   ☐ Poetry therapy
☐ Trigger management   ☐ Humor & jokes   ☐ Pictures in color
☐ Narrative therapy   ☐ Creative tasks   ☐ Journaling
☐ Shorter book   ☐ Longer book   ☐ Fun stuff
☐ More ideas:

Email this form to kimrosenthal@gmail.com or send to P.O. Box 2783, Lenoir NC 28645.

Made in the USA
Las Vegas, NV
30 March 2024

87976419R10083